OCD Digital Government Studies

Open Government Data in Mexico

THE WAY FORWARD

This work is published under the responsibility of the Secretary-General of the OECD. The opinions expressed and arguments employed herein do not necessarily reflect the official views of OECD member countries.

This document, as well as any data and any map included herein, are without prejudice to the status of or sovereignty over any territory, to the delimitation of international frontiers and boundaries and to the name of any territory, city or area.

Please cite this publication as:
OECD (2018), *Open Government Data in Mexico: The Way Forward*, OECD Digital Government Studies, OECD Publishing, Paris.
http://dx.doi.org/10.1787/9789264297944-en

ISBN 978-92-64-29793-7 (print)
ISBN 978-92-64-29794-4 (PDF)

Series: OECD Digital Government Studies
ISSN 2413-1954 (print)
ISSN 2413-1962 (online)

The statistical data for Israel are supplied by and under the responsibility of the relevant Israeli authorities. The use of such data by the OECD is without prejudice to the status of the Golan Heights, East Jerusalem and Israeli settlements in the West Bank under the terms of international law.

Photo credits: Cover © Jezael Melgoza.

Corrigenda to OECD publications may be found on line at: *www.oecd.org/about/publishing/corrigenda.htm*.

Foreword

Since 2013, the Mexican government has recognised open government data (OGD) as a policy priority. Its inclusion as a strategic tool for achieving the goals of Mexico's National Development Plan and National Digital Strategy underscores the importance of open data for the digital transformation of the Mexican public sector. Using open government data and collaborating with citizens to address society's needs and policy challenges are the cornerstones of digital government and are in line with Mexico's efforts to develop a digital economy. Moreover, OGD is an integral part of efforts to strengthen public sector productivity, accountability and integrity, to facilitate business and civic innovation, and to promote evidence-informed policy making.

Thanks to such efforts, Mexico ranks 5th in the 2017 OECD Open, Useful and Reusable Data (OURdata) Index, compared to 10th place in the 2014 pilot version. The OURdata Index assesses how well OECD countries make open data available and accessible and encourages its reuse for creating products and services.

As a follow-up to the 2016 *Open Government Data Review of Mexico*, this report was prepared at the request of the Coordination of the National Digital Strategy at the Office of the President. The purpose is to assess the implementation of the policy recommendations provided in the 2016 review. It proposes a set of strategic policy recommendations to help the Mexican government move forward in implementing its open data policy and achieve sustainable and continuous results.

The project complements the ongoing close collaboration on open government data between the OECD and the Mexican government to foster multilateral efforts and international co-operation. Mexican decision makers have regularly and actively participated in the OECD Expert Group Meeting on Open Government Data, contributed to the development of the 2017 *OECD/G20 Compendium of Good Practices on the Use of Open Data for Anti-Corruption*, and have participated as peer reviewers in OECD digital government reviews covering open data across different OECD countries and partners such as Argentina and Sweden.

This project draws upon the analytical framework for open data highlighted by the OECD working paper, *Open Government Data: Towards Empirical Analysis of Open Data Initiatives*, and on the *OECD Open Government Data Survey*. These analytical tools are framed within the work of the OECD on digital government and based on the OECD Recommendation of the Council on Digital Government Strategies.

This project also contributes to OECD Going Digital project, which aims to support governments and policy makers as they advance in the digital transformation of their public sectors, economic activities and societies overall.

Acknowledgements

This follow-up project to the 2016 *Open Government Data Review of Mexico* was prepared by the OECD Directorate for Public Governance (GOV), led by Marcos Bonturi.

It was produced by the Reform of the Public Sector Division (GOV/RPS), headed by Edwin Lau, under the supervision of Barbara-Chiara Ubaldi, Senior Project Manager and lead of the Digital Transformation of the Public Sector work.

Chapters 1, 2 and 3 were written by Jacob Arturo Rivera Perez, Digital Government and Open Data Policy Analyst (GOV/RPS). All chapters benefited from strategic contributions and revisions provided by Barbara-Chiara Ubaldi. Reginald Dadzie, Junior Consultant (GOV/RPS), provided data analytical support and contributed with sections of Chapters 2 and 3. Liv Gaunt and Javier Gonzalez provided editorial and administrative support.

The OECD is especially grateful to the following high-level public officials from Argentina, France, Korea, Spain and the United Kingdom for their participation during the webinar that was organised for the purpose of this review:

- **Mr. Gonzalo I. Iglesias,** National Director of Data and Public Information, Argentina.
- **Ms. Paula Forteza,** Parliamentarian, National Assembly of the French Republic, France.
- **Mr. Ys Lee,** Open Data Center, Agency for the National Information Society (NIA), Government of Korea.
- **Ms. Cristina Morales Puerta,** General Deputy Director for the Information Society and the Digital Agenda, Ministry of Energy, Tourism and Digital Economy, Spain.
- **Mr. Salvador Soriano,** Secretariat for the Information Society and the Digital Agenda, Ministry of Energy, Tourism and Digital Economy, Spain.
- **Ms. Pauline Ferris,** National, International and Research Group, Digital Cabinet Office, United Kingdom.
- **Mr. Thom Townsend,** Senior Policy Advisor, Digital Cabinet Office, United Kingdom.

This project benefited from support provided by the Coordination of the National Digital Strategy in Mexico, through the General Direction of Open Data, the Ministry of Public Administration, and the Research and Innovation Centre on Information and Communication Technologies (INFOTEC).

The authors are grateful for the support provided by Ambassador Mónica Aspe, Permanent Representative of Mexico to the OECD; Alejandra Lagunes, former Co-ordinator of the National Digital Strategy in Mexico; Yolanda Martinez, Co-ordinator of the National Digital Strategy in Mexico; Enrique Zapata, General Director of Open

Data, and Andrea Barenque, Deputy Director of Open Data. The OECD Secretariat is also grateful to Maya Camacho, Second Secretary from the Permanent Delegation of Mexico to the OECD for her support throughout this follow-up project.

Table of contents

Tables

Figures

Boxes

Executive summary

To ensure the long-term sustainability of Mexico's open government data (OGD) policy, it is necessary to analyse the results achieved, recognise the coming challenges and identify strategic actions. Open government data is a dynamic process that requires a sound and agile governance framework that provides institutional stability. Political leadership is also needed to support the development of a mature data-driven public sector.

Since the 2016 OECD *Open Government Data Review of Mexico*, Mexico has made real progress. However, it needs to improve its overall governance context to sustain further efforts and build a solid basis for continuous and sustainable policy implementation. This means not only assessing the institutional, legal and regulatory frameworks, but also identifying adequate funding models, reinforcing strategic leadership and the understanding of open data, building managerial and technical capacities across public sector institutions, and adopting policy monitoring and feedback mechanisms.

This can contribute to greater data discoverability and accessibility and, in turn, bolster data reuse and contribute to good governance, social inclusion, public sector productivity, social engagement, and data-driven business innovation.

Whenever feasible, the Mexican government's strategic actions should be the result of collaboration involving stakeholders from the public, private and third sectors, the media and academia. Such collaboration can help secure high demand from potential data re-users, as well as a sense of policy ownership and shared responsibility among public sector and non-government actors. It will also help build strong support from the OGD community, which is critical for policy sustainability. This approach would also strengthen feedback mechanisms to better monitor and track user demand and impact.

Main findings

Mexico has taken on board the recommendations from the 2016 review; most have either been implemented, initiated or are under discussion. Efforts should now be focused on improvements in the federal government and the public sector as a whole, such as:

- ensuring sustainable institutional governance, policy funding, and high-level political support for OGD
- structuring policy implementation
- sustaining efforts to build awareness among public officials on the strategic value of open data for developing better policies and services
- promoting the use of the open data portal as a platform for multi-stakeholder collaboration and sustained data demand
- developing policy monitoring, feedback and oversight mechanisms.

Key recommendations

The Government of Mexico is encouraged to:

- Strengthen the institutional governance of open government data policy by creating and formalising the positions of a chief data officer and chief digital transformation officer, and consider the creation of a digitalisation agency in charge of co-ordinating the country's digital agenda.
- Ensure the regular flow of funds to implement open data policy and support open data initiatives across key public sector institutions. This could include greater participation by the Ministry of Finance in order to use the budget cycle and the funding of digital projects to support open data initiatives.
- Strengthen the national legal framework for open government data by developing a specific law on open government data. As a governance instrument, the purpose of this law would be to support policy continuity by setting clear regulations that improve leadership and capacities within public sector institutions to make data available and accessible and to promote the strategic reuse of data, as well as support policy monitoring and evaluation mechanisms.
- Develop a dedicated national open data roadmap, in line with the overall national digital agenda, the National Digital Strategy, and defined through an open and inclusive process. This is necessary to bring further clarity to the open data policy by defining a joint vision and setting more structured, clear and specific actions, highlighting how policy goals will be achieved and by whom (beyond the leading role of body in charge of policy co-ordination) as well as what institutions will be involved in the implementation process.
- Further connect open data initiatives with other sectoral policies and vice versa, and sustain the current efforts to use open data for anti-corruption, public procurement of major infrastructure projects, natural risk management, and social inclusion.
- Develop a more mature and strategic public sector open data ecosystem and improve data stewardship by supporting the appointment of institutional chief data officers in line ministries and ensuring inter-institutional collaboration through horizontal co-ordination bodies.
- Sustain capacity-building efforts across public sector institutions. Despite the policy achievements to date, it is necessary to increase policy maturity by developing understanding, skills and capacities across the public sector. Ensuring the sustainability of capacity-building bodies, with the appropriate financial and human resources, is crucial in this respect.
- Further develop data architecture and data governance models for the public sector, and connect these efforts to the overall open data policy. This is necessary to support streamlined inter-institutional data-sharing practices, contribute to public sector productivity and efficiency, ensure more efficient data management models, and make open government data more available and accessible, and support greater data reuse.
- Continue efforts to strengthen the value of the MX Open Data Infrastructure (IDMX) for all actors and for policy sustainability.
- Support data discoverability, availability, accessibility and reuse by: 1) improving the usefulness and user-friendliness of the central open data portal; 2) building capacities among key partners such as journalists and civil society organisations; and 3) enabling collective efforts to map the open data ecosystem. New champions should also be identified, and data demand aggregated.
- Involve major private sector players in order to make the business case for open data in Mexico and explore the implementation of government-led seed funding

models. This would contribute to the sustainability of open data policy by invigorating data demand and the sustainability of the still-emerging start-up ecosystem.

- Develop and implement open-by-default mechanisms to support policy monitoring, reporting, feedback, and adaptability. Open monitoring mechanisms (e.g. dashboards and rankings) and feedback exercises would improve public sector accountability, monitor users' needs and demand in relation to OGD policy, and boost more evidence-informed policy making.

Chapter 1. Introduction:
The 2016 *Open Government Data Review of Mexico*

This chapter provides an overview of the state of open government data in Mexico until 2015. It aims to provide and discuss the main achievements of, and challenges faced by, the Mexican government in relation to the definition and implementation of its open government data policy with relation to OECD's analytical framework and measurement tools for open government data policies, centring on six core areas of analysis, as presented in the 2016 Open Government Data Review of Mexico.

In June 2016, the OECD published the *Open Government Data Review of Mexico* (OECD, 2016). The review was carried out at the request of the Office of the President of Mexico (Presidencia de la República), through the Coordination of the National Digital Strategy (Coordinación de la Estrategia Digital Nacional, CEDN). It also benefited from close collaboration with the Mexican Ministry of Public Administration (Secretaría de la Función Pública, SFP).

The purpose of the 2016 review was to assess the state of open government data in Mexico by 2015 and foster peer learning among public sector officials. For such a purpose, an OECD peer review mission was organised to the country in November 2015. The peer review mission and the final review benefited from the participation of and advice provided by the peers from France (represented by the French Task Force for Open Data, ETALAB, at the Prime Minister's Secretariat-General for Modernisation of Public Action), and Korea (represented by officials from the Public Data Policy Division at the Ministry of the Interior, and the Korean Open Data Centre at the National Information Society Agency, NIA). Their insights helped the Mexican government to move the open government data policy forward in the country in line with best practices among these and other leading OECD countries.

The analysis centred on reviewing the key institutional, organisational, legal, regulatory, cultural, and technical challenges faced by the Mexican government, and discussing how the aforementioned challenges hindered the availability, accessibility and reuse of open government data towards the co-creation of greater good governance, the social and economic value in the country.

The review benefited from the administration of a survey across actors from the public, private and third sectors in Mexico. Additional data provided by the Mexican government and collected through the OECD Open Government Data Survey in 2013/14, was also useful to better assess and understand the evolution of open government data in Mexico. OECD policy measurement instruments such as the pilot version of the Open, Useful and Reusable Data (OURdata) Index – published in 2014 – guided the analytical work of the OECD and helped appraise the Mexican open government data policy in relation to other OECD countries.

Mexico's involvement in OECD regional policy reviews covering open government data, such as the 2014 OECD report, *Open Government in Latin America* (OECD, 2014), also enriched the wealth of data and knowledge on Mexico's efforts on open government data prior to the publication of the Executive Decree in 2015.

The review also benefited from the active engagement of Mexico in OECD fora such as the Expert Group Meeting on Open Government Data and the OECD Working Party of Senior Officials on Digital Government (E-Leaders). These fora enable the exchange of best practices between OECD countries and strategic partners towards mutual learning. Practices from leading OECD countries were used as examples throughout the review in order to enable the transference and adaptation of successful international policy practices to the Mexican context.

Mexico in the context of the OECD work on open government data

Collaboration efforts between the OECD and the Mexican government in relation to open government data comprise different milestones, including:

1. The publication of the 2016 *Open Government Data Review of Mexico.*

2. The publication of the *OECD/G20 Compendium of Good Practices on the Use of Open Data for Anti-Corruption* within the framework of the G20 Anti-Corruption Working Group.
3. The first, second and third versions of the OECD Open Government Data Survey, for which data collection took place in 2013, 2014 and 2016/2017, respectively. These data served as the evidence basis for the development of the first pilot version of the OURdata Index, published in 2014, and its 2017 edition.

Results from the 2014 pilot of the OURdata Index (OECD, 2015) placed Mexico among the top ten OECD countries in regard to the definition and implementation of OGD policies (see Figure 1.1).

While data collection for the 2014 OURdata Index took place before the peer review mission to Mexico City (November 2015), results for the 2014 Index showed early signs of the advancements of the Mexican government in regard to open government data. For instance, earlier achievements such as the 2013 beta version of the central open government data portal, the creation of the open data taskforce (known as the Open Data Squad) and the implementation of public consultation efforts to better inform and prioritise the publication of OGD were key milestones that paved the way towards greater efforts to spur OGD-driven public value creation.

Figure 1.1. 2014 OECD Open, Useful, Reusable Government Data (OURdata) Index

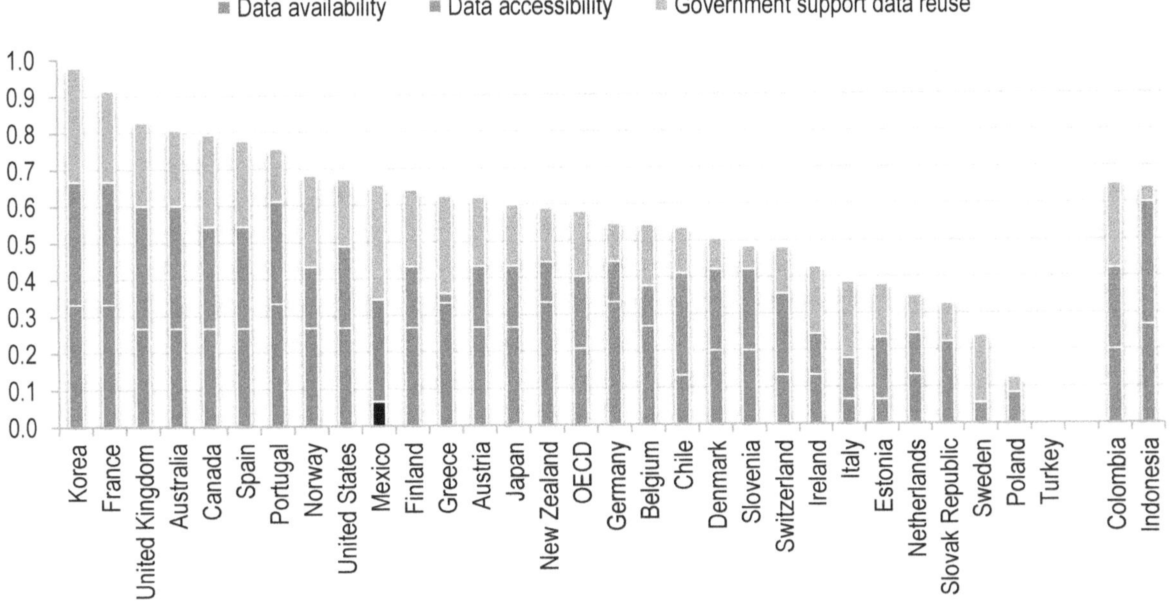

Note: Data for the Czech Republic, Hungary, Iceland, Israel and Luxembourg are not available. Turkey does not have a national ODG portal. Data for Indonesia are for 2015. The 2014 Index is a "pilot" version covering the following dimensions: data accessibility and data availability on the national data portal, and government's efforts to support data reuse.
Source: OECD (2015), "Open government data", in *Government at a Glance 2015*, OECD Publishing, Paris, http://dx.doi.org/10.1787/gov_glance-2015-48-en.

Yet, the 2017 edition of the OURdata Index (see Figure 1.2) provides strong evidence of the advancements achieved by the Mexican government in regard to open government data since the publication of the 2014 pilot version of the Index. This evolution results from the sustained and continuous efforts on open government data implemented by the Office of the President in Mexico from 2015 to 2017.

Results from the 2017 OUR data Index indicate that significant efforts have been made in Mexico to support open government data reuse in order to build the basis for the further co-creation of good governance, economic and social returns. In particular, great efforts were invested in different initiatives and programmes to promote data reuse and increase open data literacy among different user communities. These actions contributed to Mexico's second position in relation to Pillar 3 of the 2017 OURdata Index (government's support for the reuse of open government data).

Figure 1.2. 2017 OECD Open Useful Reusable Government Data (OURdata) Index

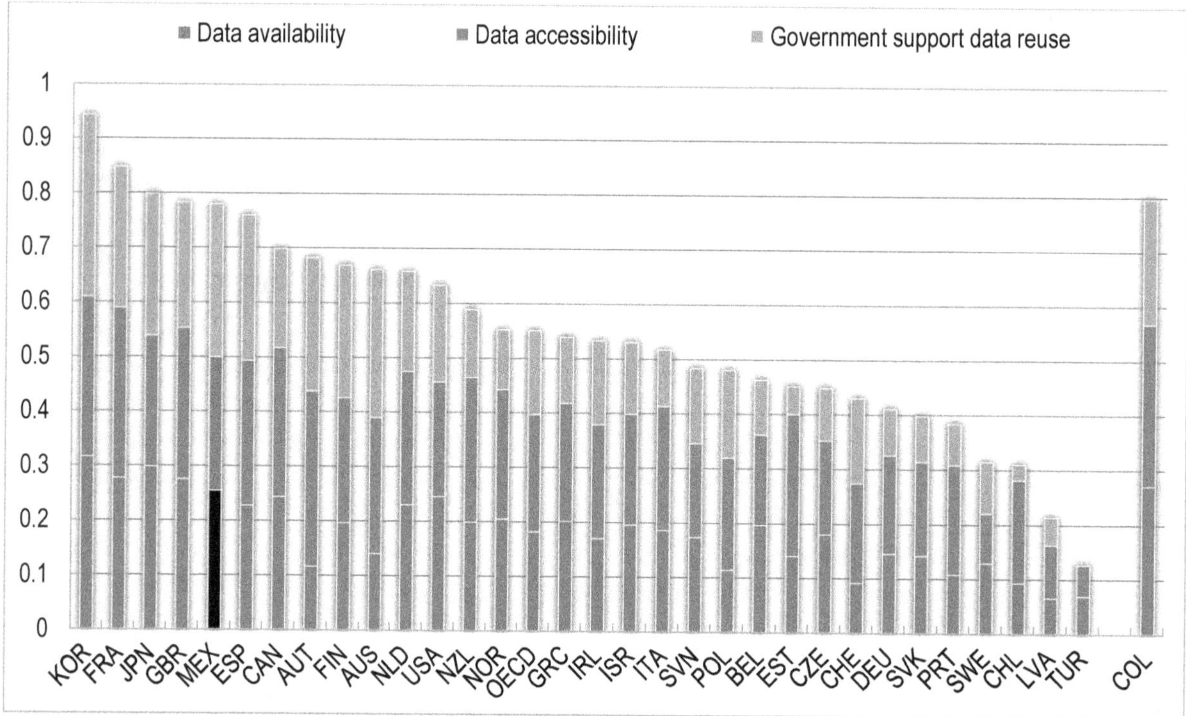

Note: Data for Hungary, Iceland and Luxembourg are not available. Denmark does not have a central/federal data portal and therefore is not displayed in the Index. Information on data for Israel: http://dx.doi.org/10.1787/888932315602.
Source: OECD (2017), *Government at a Glance 2017*, OECD Publishing, Paris, http://dx.doi.org/10.1787/gov_glance-2017-en.

Initiatives such as Prospera Digital & Misalud[1] have improved social and digital inclusion, public service delivery and efficiency, and promoted better outcomes in terms of maternal and infant health.[2] New open-data-related businesses have emerged in Mexico and new digital products and services supporting more efficient decision making and planning were created through the reuse of open government data. Initiatives such as Labora (see "Open data and the data-driven economy" in Chapter 2.) promoted data-driven entrepreneurship, which is expected to have a positive impact on data-driven business innovation.

Tracing the path of open government data in Mexico

Since 2014, the overall institutional, legal and policy governance for open government data matured as a result of high-level political commitment and the leadership of the CEDN within the Office of the President. This contributed to the development of a more advantageous pro-open data environment in the country.

On the one hand, the leadership of the CEDN, through the General Direction of Open Data, and the operational support provided by the Ministry of Public Administration, through the Digital Government Unit, have been critical in spurring the development of open data initiatives across the central and local levels in Mexico since 2013.

In parallel, the operational role of the Ministry of the Public Administration was helpful in ensuring inter-institutional co-ordination. The ministry chairs the Sub-Commission of Open Data (Subcomisión de Datos Abiertos), which is composed of data administrators from public sector institutions. As a sub-body of the Inter-Ministerial Commission for E-Government Development (Comisión Intersecretarial para el Desarrollo del Gobierno Electrónico, CIDGE), the Sub-Commission connects the work on open government data to digital government policies and the overall digital transformation of the public sector in Mexico.

The availability of key legal and regulatory instruments, such as the 2015 Executive Decree on Open Data (Government of Mexico, 2015a) and the 2015 General Law on Transparency (Government of Mexico, 2015b) (which integrated the concept of open data), strengthen the legal foundations of open government data in the country. Earlier legal instruments, such as the 2011 Agreement on the Interoperability Framework and Open Data for the Federal Public Administration, also contributed to paving the way for the development of the open data policy since 2012.

The identification of open data as a key enabler of the National Digital Strategy (Government of Mexico, 2013), provided an ideal policy framework to connect open government data to broader policy goals such as public sector modernisation and the 2013-18 National Development Plan (see Figure 1.3).

Efforts to better guide data governance within the Mexican public sector were also developed as a result of the open government data policy. The CEDN developed the first version of the Implementation Guide of the Open Data Policy (Guía de Implementación de la Política de Datos Abiertos) (Government of Mexico, 2015c) to help institutions define and implement their institutional plans to open up government data.

The INEGI (the National Statistics Office) developed the Open Data Technical Norm for National Interest Information, and its accompanying technical implementation guide, covering key aspects of the data value chain such as the use of the Data Catalogue Vocabulary (DCAT standard) for metadata provision.

Supporting the implementation of all of the above-mentioned data governance instruments was one of the key goals of the Open Data Squad (Escuadrón de Datos Abiertos). The Squad, a taskforce created by the General Direction of Open Data, provides guidance and training to public officials throughout the data publication process prior to the availability of data on the central open government data portal, datos.gob.mx.

Figure 1.3. Policy framework of Mexico's open government data policy

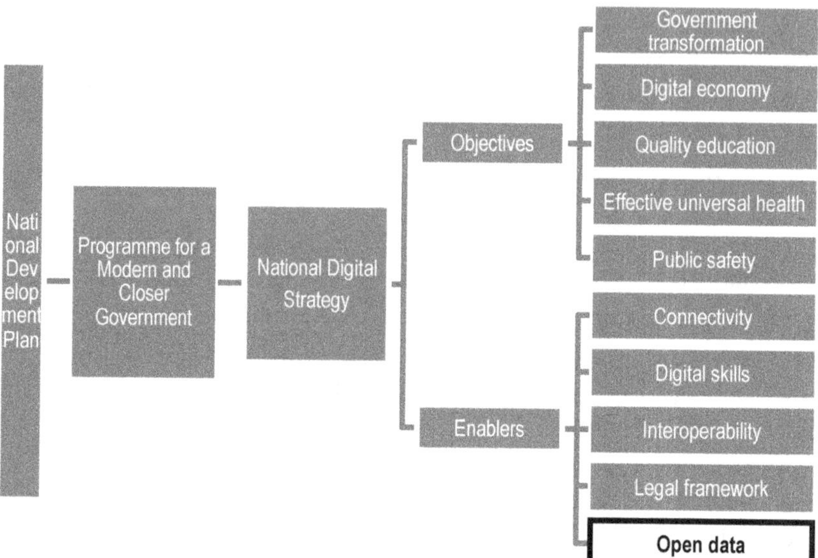

Source: OECD (2016), *Open Government Data Review of Mexico: Data Reuse for Public Sector Impact and Innovation*, OECD Publishing, Paris, http://dx.doi.org/10.1787/9789264259270-en.

The General Direction for Open Data followed a dynamic and flexible human capital procurement model that enabled bringing on board external consultants and experts (e.g. on data analysis and data science) to perform specific projects. These projects are performed under the leadership of the General Director for Open Data (one of the few fixed job positions part of the civil service within this office) and the Co-ordinator of the National Digital Strategy.

As a result of the above, the General Direction for Open Data worked as a data lab *de facto* where open data initiatives were designed, tested, implemented and matured. Initiatives such as the development of the Strategic Open Data Infrastructure, the Public Challenges initiative (Retos Públicos), Labora, DataLab, the implementation of the Open Data Charter's Anticorruption Open Up Guide, and the Open Mexico Network (Red México Abierto) (see Box 1.1) are the result of these efforts.

Box 1.1. Open data initiatives developed by the Mexican government between 2012-16

Since 2013, the chief data officer (CDO) has implemented open data initiatives aiming to deliver policy results in compliance with the responsibilities set by the Open Data Executive Decree and with the ambitions embedded in the National Open Data Policy:

- In 2015, a public consultation process was launched to inform the prioritisation of data disclosure by public institutions at the central level. This exercise was useful to create the Strategic Open Data Infrastructure (Infraestructura Estratégica de Datos Abiertos, IEDA). The definition of the Infrastructure (i.e. a group of datasets that have been prioritised by the central government for release due to its potential contribution to national development goals) has been crucial to guide open data disclosure by public institutions.

Box 1.1. Open data initiatives developed by the Mexican government between 2012-16
(continued)

- The Open Data Squads (Escuadrones de Datos Abiertos, ODSs) were created to provide technical and regulatory guidance and support from the centre of government to central and local public institutions. The work of the ODSs has been instrumental to build capacities for data management (i.e. production, exchange, publication and use) towards greater OGD disclosure on the central portal. Their work goes hand in hand with the technical expertise offered by the National Statics Office (the INEGI), which has been in charge of developing and publishing technical guidelines and norms for open data disclosure. All these efforts help public institutions to follow the guidelines included in the Implementation Guide of the Open Data Policy (Guía de Implementación de la Política de Datos Abiertos), which aims to assist them in developing and implementing their own institutional open data plans and to disclose open data based on a demand-driven approach.

- Retos Públicos, an initiative that provides incentives for app development, has been useful to connect developers and public institutions in order to foster collaboration around specific policy issues and sectors. As a result, web- and mobile-based platforms and apps have been developed by private sector organisations to improve public service delivery or to tackle citizens' information access asymmetry. Other resulting tools are good examples of the use of digital technologies and open data for risk management, hence linking open data initiatives with the achievement of the Sustainable Development Goals.

- Mexico's efforts on open data are not limited to the central level. The CEDN and the SFP designed and implemented the Open Mexico Network (Red Mexico Abierto) to bring local governments closer to the national open data policy. The OMN has been useful not only to enable greater local OGD disclosure on the central portal, and to spur open data initiatives at the local level, but also to ensure the development of local open data initiatives coherent with the national policy. The network has been equally useful to bring local governments in Mexico closer to international open data instruments, such as the International Open Data Charter, thereby drawing a direct link between the international open data community and local governments, and enhancing multi-level policy coherence around open data.

- Open Data 100 (the Mexican chapter of Open Data 500) aims to map the use of open government data by social and, more importantly, by private sector organisations. This initiative (developed in collaboration with the GovLab of the University of New York) has enabled the Mexican government to identify business-oriented user communities within the OGD ecosystem using OGD, thus paving the way to strengthening the capacities to measure the economic value created through OGD reuse by private sector organisations.

Source: OECD (2016), *Open Government Data Review of Mexico: Data Reuse for Public Sector Impact and Innovation*, OECD Publishing, Paris, http://dx.doi.org/10.1787/9789264259270-en.

Main challenges identified in 2015

The experimental test-and-learn approach implemented by the Office of the President allowed enough flexibility to design and implement open government data initiatives and advance the OGD agenda in the country. Nevertheless, key challenges remained at the very core of the Mexican public sector in regard to the normalisation of open government data as a common practice among public sector institutions (in particular, line ministries), and the co-creation of public value.

Results for the *Open Government Data Review of Mexico* identified six key areas of work to be prioritised by the Mexican government in this regard (OECD, 2016):

Area 1: Governance: Building a pro-open-data public sector

- In 2015, the Mexican open government data policy was relatively new. It benefited from: 1) high-level political support (reflected by the Executive Decree); and 2) an institutional governance framework (shared by the Office of the President and the SFP) that enabled the delivery of quick policy wins. However, such an institutional governance model risked, and still does, the sustainability of the OGD policy in the mid and long term; thus, the vast majority of those policy wins were achieved under the leadership of, and the support provided by, the Office of the President (namely the General Direction of Open Data). As a result, the continuity and permanence of this clear institutional visionary leadership will play a key role in the sustainability and impact of the OGD policy.
- The lack of maturity of the open data ecosystem inside the public sector exacerbated the above-mentioned scenario. Public sector institutions, with some exceptions, were struggling to fully understand, internalise and put OGD into practice. Increasing data stewardship within public sector institutions (e.g. institutional chief open data officers) was of utter importance to move away from the transparency-oriented, technical, bureaucratic and reactive approach guiding open government data at the time. The vision for OGD inside the Office of the President was not echoed by the broad public sector.
- Despite the implementation of Retos Públicos, and few clear examples of the use of open government data to address key broader policy challenges in the country (e.g. fight against corruption and reduction of maternal mortality), the OGD policy lacked a clear strategy or action plan defining policy milestones, strategic areas of work, policy priorities, and key actors in charge of advancing the OGD agenda. Peer learning and openness to the international open data ecosystem contributed to building the knowledge base for OGD within the Office of the President, but a clear path for action was absent, therefore affecting a more structured policy implementation.
- Streamlining the legal and regulatory governance for privacy and data protection, under the leadership and legally based responsibility of the National Institute of Transparency, Access to Information and Personal Data Protection (INAI), was needed to bring clarity in regard to the limits, responsibilities and liabilities of freedom of information, personal privacy and data protection regulations.

Area 2: Towards a demand- and value-driven data disclosure

- The development of the Strategic Open Data Infrastructure exemplified the willingness of the Mexican government to prioritise and guide the publication of open government data. However, the centralisation of consultation efforts by the Office of the President - and the lack of efforts across public sector institutions to run consultation exercises – undermined the further implementation of a systemic open by default, demand- and user-driven approach supporting data publication and policy making.
- The unavailability of online, streamlined and efficient instruments in place to request open government data exacerbated the above-mentioned scenario. The functions of the central OGD portal were limited in this regard, and the process to request OGD was constrained by complicated and time-consuming processes to request and access public sector information.

Area 3: Building skills across non-institutional user communities and engaging the ecosystem

- Retos Públicos set a precedent as an example of multi-stakeholder collaboration, value co-creation, and the co-design of citizen-government solutions to policy challenges. Yet, despite the involvement of some line ministries, user engagement was still limited and, sometimes, restricted to the usual suspects of the Mexican public sector transparency and open data ecosystem. In particular, Retos Públicos faced funding challenges undermining its sustainability.
- Notwithstanding the political, social and policy relevance of anti-corruption efforts in Mexico, and the role OGD played in this regard, key actors were left aside on consultation exercises, namely data-driven journalists and civil society organisations working on civic tech.

Area 4: Open data and the data-driven economy

- While the economic discourse supporting the OGD policy in the country was high on the agenda, the ecosystem was still too immature to fully benefit from the value of OGD for economic development and entrepreneurship despite the presence of some frontrunner small- and medium-sized enterprises (SMEs) capitalising on OGD. For this reason, it was necessary to define and implement collaboration exercises, and capacity-building initiatives targeting data enthusiasts and data-driven entrepreneurs. Policy coherence was crucial in this respect.
- One of the main challenges was to create a data-driven business community capable of capitalising on the value of open data (including, but not restricted to OGD). The definition of public-private-academic partnerships was necessary to invigorate the ecosystem, create skills and contribute to the data-driven and knowledge economy.

Area 5: Towards a data-driven public sector

- The Mexican government struggled to acknowledge the role of public sector institutions as data *prosumers* – meaning not only as data producers but also as data consumers. In this regard, it was necessary to connect open government data to the overall data governance model of the Mexican public sector in order to use the OGD policy as an enabler of more efficient and streamlined inter-institutional data-sharing practices.

- There was also clear potential to respond to public sector institution demands in terms of the development of skills and capacities for data analysis, data science and big data. The construction of a data-driven smart government and public sector intelligence, aligned with digital government and open government data policies, emerged as a policy area of untapped potential for the digital transformation of the Mexican public sector.

Area 6: Open data at the local level

- Further reaching and engaging local governments and actors was among the key priorities of the General Direction of Open Data and the Ministry of Public Administration. Yet, as a country with a federal government model, Mexico faced multi-level governance challenges affecting multi-level policy implementation and co-ordination.
- The Open Mexico Network aimed to connect the central OGD policy with local efforts and the local ecosystem of actors. Nonetheless, there was room for manoeuvre to further use this platform as a horizontal co-ordination forum between local governments in order to build systemic knowledge based on peer learning, the exchange of successful best practices, and lessons from failure.
- The platform also offered an opportunity to further connect and inter-connect local practices and practitioners with the achievement of supranational policy goals such as the Sustainable Development Goals, and the Extractive Industries Transparency Initiative (EITI).[3]

Notes

1. For more information, see www.gob.mx/misalud.

2. The release of 500 different datasets on maternal mortality and its effects helped government officials and different stakeholders to produce new insights to improve maternal and infant health. These insights subsequently led to the creation of Prospera Digital, a pilot programme that provides a two-way information exchange platform between users and those 326 health clinics adhered to the programme. Evidence collected through the Open Government Data Survey 3.0 shows that through this programme more than 130 maternal emergency cases have been addressed and that 437 932 text messages from adherents have been sent to participating health clinics. The programme has now been institutionalised across the Mexican territory with the name misalud.

3. For more information, visit https://eiti.org/.

References

Government of Mexico (2015a), "Decreto por el que se Establece la Regulación en Materia de Datos Abiertos" [Open Data Executive Order], *Diario Oficial de la Federación*, 20 February, www.dof.gob.mx/nota_detalle.php?codigo=5382838&fecha=20/02/2015.

Government of Mexico (2015b), "Ley General de Transparencia y Acceso a la Información Pública" [General Law on Transparency and Access to Public Information], *Diario Oficial de la Federación*, 4 May, www.dof.gob.mx/nota_detalle.php?codigo=5391143&fecha=04/05/2015.

Government of Mexico (2015c), "Guía de Implementación de la Política de Datos Abiertos" [Implementation Guide of the Open Data Policy], http://datos.gob.mx/guia.

Government of Mexico (2013), "Estrategia Digital Nacional" [National Digital Strategy], November, http://cdn.mexicodigital.gob.mx/EstrategiaDigital.pdf.

OECD (2017), *Government at a Glance 2017*, OECD Publishing, Paris, http://dx.doi.org/10.1787/gov_glance-2017-en.

OECD (2016), *Open Government Data Review of Mexico: Data Reuse for Public Sector Impact and Innovation*, OECD Publishing, Paris, http://dx.doi.org/10.1787/9789264259270-en.

OECD (2015), "Open government data", in *Government at a Glance 2015*, OECD Publishing, Paris, http://dx.doi.org/10.1787/gov_glance-2015-48-en.

OECD (2014), *Open Government in Latin America*, OECD Publishing, Paris, http://dx.doi.org/10.1787/9789264223639-en.

Chapter 2. Assessing the implementation of the OECD 2016 recommendations

This chapter discusses the overall status of implementation of the policy recommendations provided by the OECD Secretariat within the framework of the 2016 OECD Open Government Data Review of Mexico. It takes into consideration the state of the open government data policy as of December 2017. It draws upon the six core areas of work discussed in Chapter 1 and the additional evidence and data collected during the peer review mission that took place for the purpose of this follow-up project. It aims to inform the additional policy recommendations discussed in Chapter 3.

The 2016 *Open Government Data Review of Mexico* provided a set of policy recommendations to the Mexican government that aimed to help the central government advance and mature the open government data policy in the country. The overall goal of these recommendations was to move open government data and public sector innovation from the edge to the core of the Mexican public sector, therefore, positioning it as the day-to-day business of policy making and public management in the country.

This chapter assesses the efforts of the Mexican government to implement the recommendations of the review since its publication in June 2016. It benefited from the additional evidence collected by the OECD Secretariat through the peer review mission held in Mexico City in October 2017 within the framework of this follow-up project.

While issues related to governance and funding are briefly discussed in this chapter, Chapter 3. explores more in detail the governance arrangements and funding models for open government data in Mexico and across OECD countries. This has the objective of providing greater policy insights and detailed policy recommendations resulting from the evidence collected during the 2017 OECD peer review mission and the survey that was administered for the purpose of this project.

The following sections present the efforts carried out by the Mexican government to put in place strategic actions for the implementation of the policy recommendations provided by the OECD. These actions (when taken) are aligned with the main challenges mentioned in Chapter 1. and were analysed in line with the following rationale:

- The recommendations are presented, assessed and discussed on a case-by-case basis. When feasible, specific recommendations were grouped based on the availability of strong connections between their content and the set of actions taken by the Mexican government.
- When assessed and depending on the information and evidence available, each case provides:

  1. the specific recommendation, or group or recommendations, provided by the OECD Secretariat
  2. the actions taken by the Mexican government (depending on the status of implementation of the recommendation)
  3. the status of the implementation of the recommendation.

The status of the implementation of each recommendation was assessed using a scorecard approach based on the following rankings defined by the OECD Secretariat:

- **Fully achieved**: Strategic actions were taken at all levels to fully address the key challenges affecting the objective of the recommendation. No further action is expected in the short, medium and long terms, but efforts should be sustained.

- **Ongoing actions**: Actions have been taken to address the recommendations. Further actions can contribute to support policy results in the long term.
- **Discussions underway on course of action**: Potential actions have been discussed by top decision makers, but the final course of action is yet to be defined and implemented.
- **Pending discussions**: Neither ongoing discussions have taken place nor has a clear course of action been defined.

Table 2.1 presents a summary of the results of the above-mentioned assessment drawing upon the evidence presented throughout the following sections.

Table 2.1. Results of the policy assessment: General summary

	Fully achieved	Ongoing actions	Discussions underway on course of action	Pending discussions
Governance: Building a pro-open-data public sector				
Recommendation 1		●		
Recommendation 2		●		
Recommendation 3			●	
Recommendation 4		●		
Recommendation 5		●		
Recommendation 6				●
Recommendation 7	●			
Towards a demand -and value-driven data disclosure				
Recommendation 1	●			
Recommendation 2	●			
Recommendation 3		●		
Building skills across external social user communities and engaging the ecosystem				
Recommendation 1	●			
Recommendation 2	●			
Recommendation 3	●			
Open data and the data-driven economy				
Recommendation 1	●			
Recommendation 2	●			
Recommendation 3				●
Towards a data-driven public sector				
Recommendation 1		●		
Recommendation 2	●			
Recommendation 3	●			
Recommendation 4		●		
Open data at the local level				
Recommendation 1	●			
Recommendation 2	●			
Recommendation 3	●			
Recommendation 4	●			
Total	14	7	1	2

Governance: Building a pro-open-data public sector

The 2016 review provided a total of seven policy recommendations aiming to strengthen the overall governance and institutional capacities for open government data in Mexico.

Recommendation 1

Sustain the co-ordination of the OGD policy implementation between the Office of the President and the SFP in the medium (three years) and long term (five years) to ensure the continuity of high-level political support for policy development and more effective policy implementation.

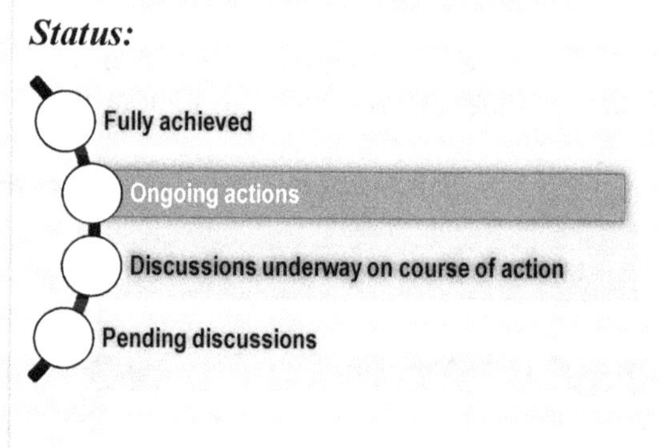

Actions taken

Since 2015, the Mexican government has taken specific actions to define a clear governance framework supporting the open data policy including, for instance, creating the provisions on open data included in the General Transparency Law, publishing the Executive Decree on Open Data, and developing the Open Data Implementation guide. Altogether, the aforementioned instruments establish regulatory pillars that support the open data policy in Mexico.

In terms of institutional governance, the Executive Decree set out clear institutional responsibilities in terms of policy co-ordination shared between Coordination of the National Digital Strategy within the Office of the President and the Digital Government Unit within the Ministry of Public Administration. As such, the institutional model has been sustained since the publication of the 2016 review.

Yet, the Mexican government is currently exploring options to reinforce the institutional model in order to contribute to the long-term sustainability, continuity and resilience of the open data policy and initiatives across political cycles. These efforts are aligned with OECD country experience, where changes in the administration have led to a lack of clarity on the future and/or endangered the continuity of the open data policies.

This report results from close collaboration between the OECD and Mexico in line with the willingness of the Mexican government to explore successful institutional governance arrangements for open government data policies across OECD countries. It adds up to additional efforts implemented by the Mexican government in collaboration with other organisations such as the Inter-American Development Bank (IADB).

This follow-up project aims to provide the Mexican government with a knowledge basis on how sound governance models and institutional arrangements support the open data policy in the long run. The full achievement of this recommendation is dependent on the sustainability and development of a sound institutional governance model for open data policy and the sustained implementation of efforts across administrations' efforts in line with the timeframe that was set for the recommendation in the long term (five years).

The results and recommendations of this report seek to contribute to increasing the governance maturity of the open government data policy, to its continuity, and the long-term sustainability and successful implementation in Mexico. This specific recommendation is further discussed in Chapter 3. .

Recommendation 2

Ensure the availability and continuity of federal funding for the open data policy to ensure the development and implementation of open data initiatives by the centre of government.

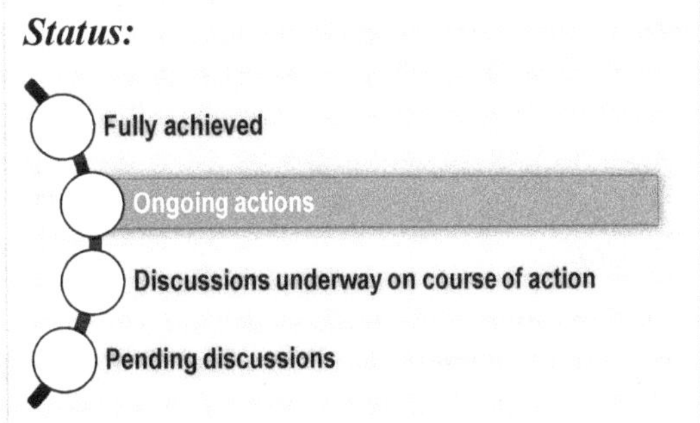

Actions taken

The Mexican Office of the President does not have a dedicated budget that can be used to finance public sector projects. As a result, it was observed in 2016 that the financing model of the open government data policy in Mexico - for all initiatives implemented by the Office of the President - was the result of funding granted by the Ministry of Communications and Transport (Secretaría de Comunicaciones y Transportes, SCT). These funds are part of the e-Mexico Trust Fund (also known as the Fideicomiso 2058) and have a cut-off date set for May 2018.

The current governance framework for open government data limits the possibility of defining dedicated funding models that would make specific financing for open data initiatives constantly available in the short term and which would help deal with financing uncertainty in the long run. Evidence collected by the OECD Secretariat during the OECD peer review to Mexico confirmed that the Ministry of Public Administration, in co-operation with the Coordination of the National Digital Strategy and the Ministry of Communications and Transport can extend the availability of the allocated resources until late 2018/early 2019. These resources are, and have been, essential to enable advances in the implementation of the open data policy. However, the lack of certainty in terms of their regular availability endangers the continuity of open data initiatives designed and directly implemented by the Office of the President in the medium and long terms. This would be particularly negative for some of the more strategic initiatives – such as the Open Data Squads and technical viability of the open data platforms – that have played a key role in developing open data capacities and awareness needed to support effective implementation across the public sector.

The absence of secured dedicated financial resources, allocated to the open data policy on a regular and permanent basis (e.g. as part of the budgeting and fiscal year cycle, or the creation of a dedicated fund) would make the reliability of funding for long-term sustainability even more critical given the current organisational model for OGD in Mexico, as it would be entirely exposed to political cycles.

Recommendation 3

Develop a structured national open data strategy in order to ground policy directives, vision, and goals, building on the needs of the national open data ecosystem. This could also help ensure the stability of the OGD governance framework in the long term.

Status:

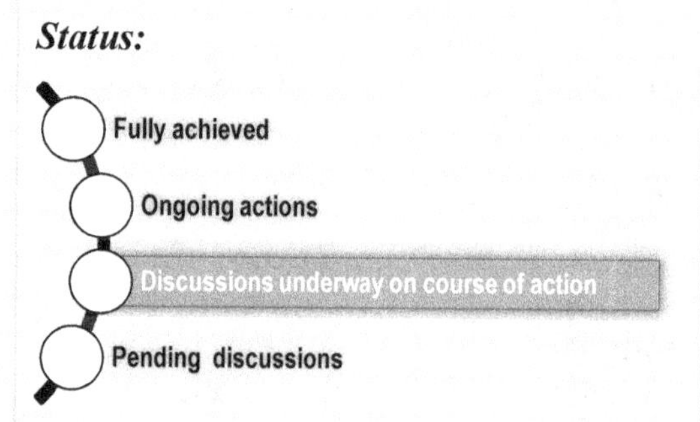

Actions taken

The inclusion of open data as one of the five key enablers of the National Digital Strategy, and the inclusion of specific action lines on open data as part of the Modern Government Programme (MGP) set general and specific goals related to open government data to be met by the Coordination of the National Digital Strategy (CEDN). Other legal and regulatory instruments such as the Open Data Executive Decree outlined policy priorities to be met by the CEDN, including data-driven economic development, competitiveness, innovation, transparency, accountability, government efficiency and better public services.

The above-mentioned objectives and lines of action set forth the path and guided the design and implementation of open data initiatives that, together, made up a *de facto* open data strategy since 2015. However, there is still room for improvement in terms of grounding policy goals and bringing further clarity to how those goals are operationalised in practice.

In the Mexican context, with open data being an inherent element of the National Digital Strategy and the MGP, the development of a dedicated open data strategy is not a viable option (from a formal point of view). However, despite the limits set by the Mexican context in terms of the legal basis and relationship between policy instruments (e.g. strategies, programmes) defining more specific milestones, actions, roles and responsibilities - in collaboration with the open data ecosystem (to ensure the right level of inclusiveness and engagement) and based on the evaluation of the policy results achieved so far – should be a priority to be addressed in the short- and mid-terms. This would help bring clarity, increase coherence among a set of diverse initiatives and projects, and strengthen the accountability of the different stakeholders - so much needed to achieve the expected results of a policy as horizontal and cross-cutting as open data.

This specific recommendation is further discussed in Chapter 3. , in the section entitled "From policy goals to a structured path: Developing an open data roadmap".

Recommendation 4

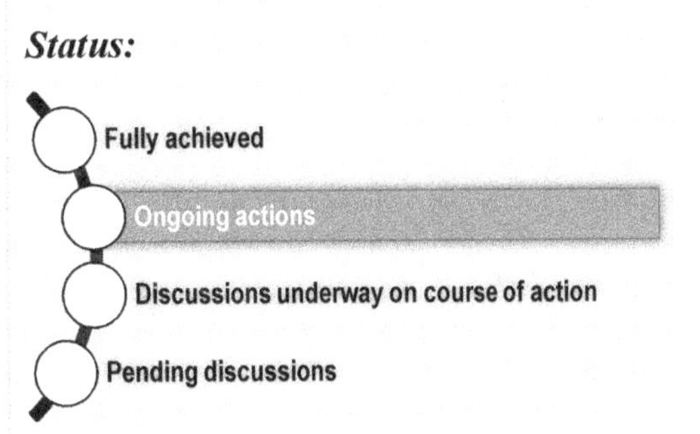

Assess the national context and the capacities of the ecosystem, *and further involve key public sector institutions (such as those in charge of sectoral policy co-ordination).*

Actions taken

On the one hand, assessing the maturity of the national open data ecosystem remains a key challenge for the Mexican government.

Earlier efforts to map OGD-driven economic activity and entrepreneurship were implemented in the context of the Open Data 100 initiative. Indeed, user-mapping exercises were continuously run within the framework of open data initiatives developed by the Office of the President. However, there is no clear evidence of any further actions taken to continue mapping the open data ecosystem more broadly in the country. The open data policy would benefit from a broader and constant user-mapping exercise, as also confirmed by the perception of actors from the private and civil sectors, who were interviewed for the purpose of this follow-up project.

In the Mexican context, the importance assigned to government openness has led to efforts to ensure unrestricted and anonymous access to open data (e.g. user registration in the portal is not mandatory in order to download OGD), but this approach restricts the collection of information to map the OGD ecosystem unless users voluntarily choose to establish communication or direct contact within the framework of other open data initiatives. In addition, low levels of public trust in government exert a negative influence affecting potential user engagement.

The General Direction of Open Data is expected to launch the Historias con Datos Initiative in March 2018, as an effort to further identify more open data users and collect information on the OGD reuse and impact of social and private OGD-driven initiatives. In light of this, in Mexico, the challenge is to sustain and implement iterating efforts and raise awareness of the need to further map the ecosystem in a proactive fashion. The open data ecosystem by itself should also self-acknowledge their role as active, not passive, policy stakeholders. Open government data requires multi-stakeholder collaboration, and in this line, all actors should be owners of the policy itself.

On the other hand, in practice, several open data initiatives have been put in place in co-ordination and collaboration with other public sector institutions beyond the initial success of the Retos Públicos initiative. Examples of this collaboration are provided in the respective following sections exploring the creation of social and economic value.

In addition, a revised version of the Implementation Guide was launched in December 2017 to continue supporting public sector institutions. The new version of the guide is the result of a consultation with public sector institutions, and it describes the revised procedures for data publication through the central portal. It also prioritises the accessibility and usefulness of open government data, therefore, focusing on improving the quality of those datasets already available on the portal. All these are important actions taken to strengthen the relevant ecosystem within the public sector, and foster open data re-use..

Recommendation 5

<table>
<tr>
<td>

Ensure the continuity of technical support bodies (such as the Open Data Squad) in order to increase data literacy inside public sector institutions.

</td>
<td>

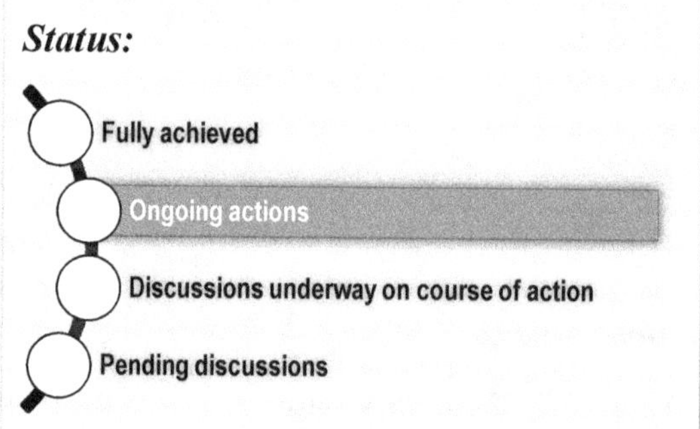

</td>
</tr>
</table>

Actions taken

The Open Data Squad (ODS) is an international best practice developed by the Coordination of National Digital Strategy and the Open Data Institute. The Squad is a taskforce within the Office of the President which provided it with a strong political lever for its activities and enough room for manoeuvre and flexibility to carry out its capacity-building work.

The work of the squad was and is linked to the willingness of the Mexican government to further build capacities across public sector institutions. Indeed, results from the survey administered for the purpose of this follow-up project show that 95 out of 124 institutions[1] are aware of the federal government efforts to increase open data and data-science-related literacy within public sector institutions, thereby highlighting the relevance of the work of the squad to support policy implementation.

Results from the survey administered for the purpose of this project show that inter-institutional data sharing and the publication of open government data are the most relevant objectives of the above-mentioned capacity-building efforts (see Figure 2.1). These findings are in line with the understanding that most public sector institutions have of open government data. Results from the survey also indicate that 93% (116 institutions)[2] understand open government data to be about opening up government data in open formats for public access and as a mechanism to increase transparency, accountability and fight corruption.

In effect, the ODS has been active since the publication of the review in 2016. The squad has solved more than 12 000 support tickets and trained roughly more than 1 000 public officials and 200 public sector institutions to open up government data since their creation in 2015.[3] It has also established self-learning hubs (using Github)[4] to increase general OGD-oriented knowledge among public officials in areas such as legal and regulatory frameworks, and data standardisation and anonymisation. However, despite these efforts, the current funding, political and governance uncertainty at the Office the President risks its permanence.

Figure 2.1. Main objectives of the capacity-building efforts for open data and data science within the public sector

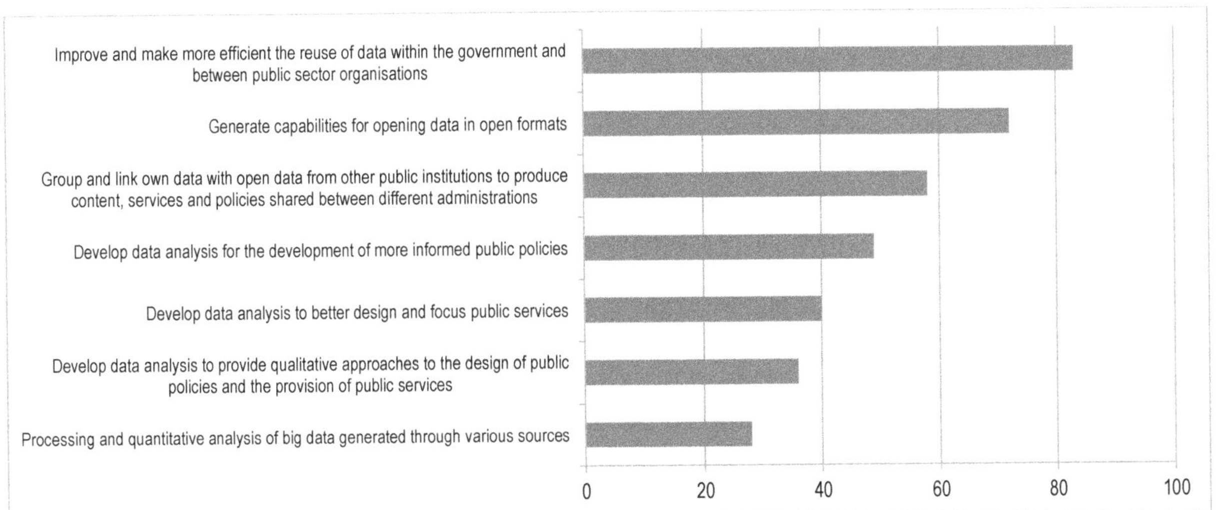

Source: Institutions' responses to OECD (2017a), "Follow-up Survey to the 2016 Open Government Data Review of Mexico", Question 5a. ¿Cuáles son las principales habilidades que dicha estrategia o política busca reforzar e incrementar?

The e-Mexico Trust Fund (See Recommendation 2 in this section on Governance) has contributed to the sustainability of the ODS in the short term by covering the salaries of consultants working in-house. However, the technical team does not have fixed contracts inside the government structure and are not part of the Mexican civil service. Although the continuity of the squad is assured towards the end of 2018, it is still highly volatile for it is contingent on regular and certain funding flow and to the stability of the institutional arrangement part of the overall governance framework in the mid and long terms. Given the extreme relevance of the squad, internationally recognised as a leading practice, it would be important to count on efforts made to ensure its permanent nature in the long run, although this may imply counting on the support of future administrations.

Recommendation 6

Highlight the relevance, and support the availability, of **institutional chief data officers** *within key public institutions. This could help to align the emerging vision for open data across public sector institutions with the central vision of the central policy co-ordinating institutions in order to exploit the value of open data to achieve sectoral policy objectives as well as broader policy goals.*

Status:

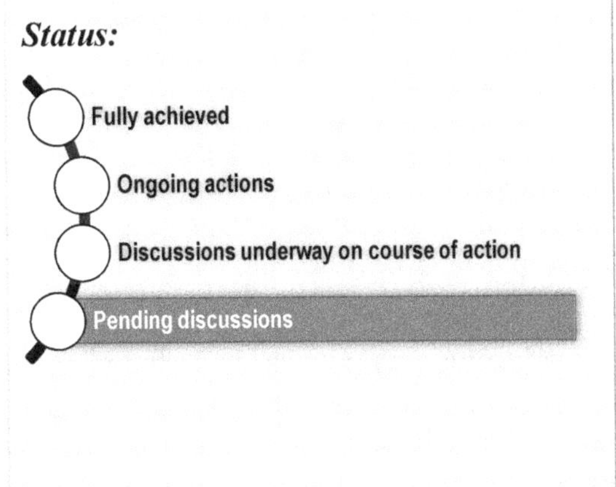

Actions taken

Despite the inter-institutional co-ordination efforts undertaken by the Ministry of Public Administration (see "Mexico in the context of the OECD work on open government data" in Chapter 1), the establishment of clear data stewardship (e.g. institutional chief data officers [iCDOs]) across the public sector remains a key challenge for the Mexican government.

The Open Data Executive Decree establishes that each government institution is responsible for the implementation of the open data policy. Nonetheless, it also establishes that institutions should comply with their current financial and human resources. This is a practice commonly supported by legal counsellors within public sector institutions in order to prevent negative impacts in the national budget, but this also limits the possibilities of establishing dedicated OGD policy implementation teams.

The Implementation Guide of the Open Data Policy (Guía de Implementación de la Política de Datos Abiertos) developed by the CEDN highlights the responsibility of public sector institutions to appoint the chiefs of staff of ministers as institutional contact points (Enlace de datos abiertos) and the technology general directors as data administrators (administradores de datos), both in charge of complying with the requirements of the Open Data Executive Decree and the Implementation Guide (e.g. including the development of open-up institutional plans).

In this line, results from the survey that was administered for the purpose of this project show that the vast majority of public sector institutions report the availability of an open-up institutional plan or open data initiative (103 out of 124).[5] Yet, results from the survey also show that the main objective pursued in most open-up institutional plans/open data initiative strategies of institutions is to increase transparency through the largest possible publication of their data (see Figure 2.2). Only 16 out of 124 institutions identified the contribution of open data to greater institutional openness (which goes beyond public sector transparency, including, for instance, user-driven approaches and user engagement), public sector accountability, and efficiency of public spending as top priorities of institutional plans. The creation of economic opportunities for the private sector (one of the top priorities of the OGD policy in Mexico) is only identified as a main policy objective by three institutions. The latter provides evidence of the transparency approach still driving open data across the public sector.

Despite the significant efforts undertaken by the current administration, the above-mentioned evidence may point to insufficient data stewardship across the Mexican public sector, which is a target that requires sustained efforts. This would be translated into the existence of clear strategic guidance and vision for the design and implementation of institutional OGD strategies that can contribute to achieving sectoral policy goals in line with broader national objectives (e.g. such as national development and the Sustainable Development Goals).

At the moment, neither the institutional contact points (mainly the chiefs of staff of public sector institutions) nor the data administrators (mainly technical level public officials), appear to have fulfilled the strategic role of institutional chief data officers. If any, the role of both the contact points and data administrators has been strongly focused on increasing data availability through the central OGD portal, and not on fully linking open data to the achievement of specific policy goals.

Figure 2.2. Main policy objectives of institutional open-up strategies

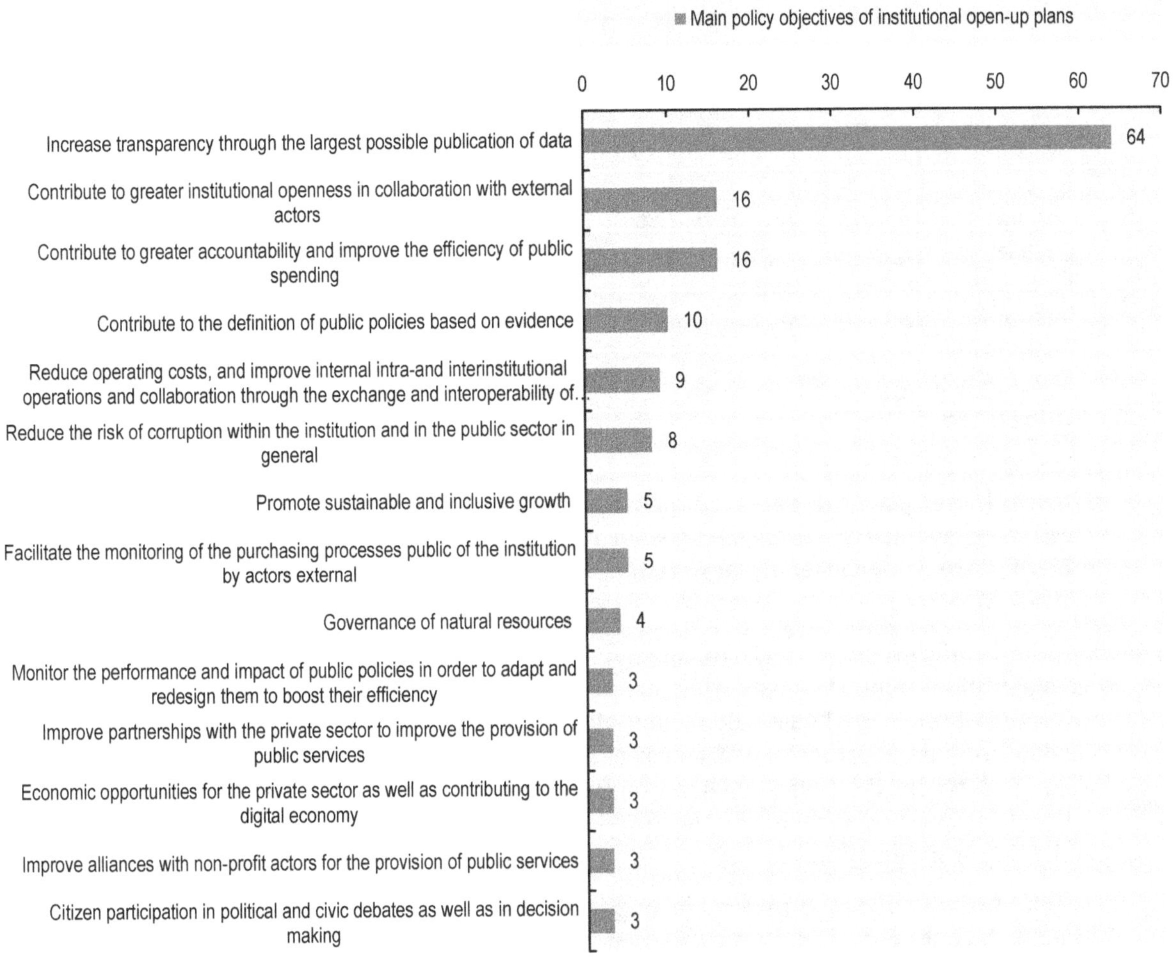

Source: Institutions' responses to OECD (2017a), "Follow-up Survey to the 2016 Open Government Data Review of Mexico", Question 8a. ¿Cuáles son los 7 objetivos principales que se persiguen con la estrategia o política pública?

In general terms, the strategic vision for open data at the Office of the President is still not widely echoed across the broad Mexican public sector to build the case to promote and, if needed, enforce the development of strategic leadership positions (such as iCDOs) as part of multi-disciplinary teams in charge of the implementation of the open data policy and its linkages with broader policy areas such as digital government, data-driven public sector and human resources development and leadership. Therefore, given the nature of the expected goals, advances would require co-ordinated efforts between different authorities (e.g. the one charged with open data co-ordination and the one responsible for human resources) and prioritisation in the short, medium and long terms.

Recommendation 7

<table>
<tr>
<td>

***Streamline data and privacy protection regulations** to reduce confusion among citizens and civil servants and decrease regulatory dispersion due to the availability of different instruments. Clear regulations regarding personal data managed by public officials are crucial to protect citizens and to increase their trust in the public sector.*

</td>
<td>

Status:

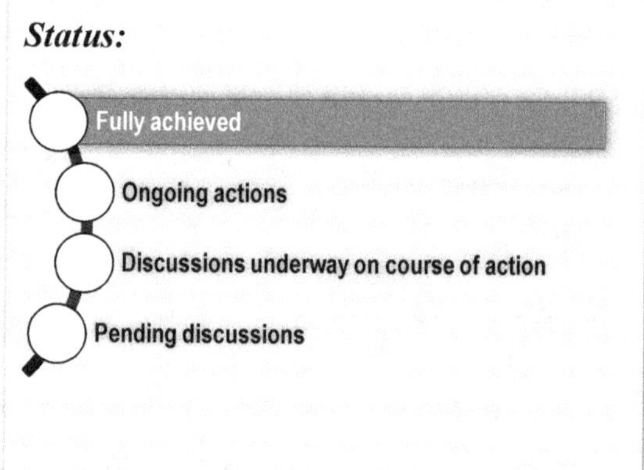

</td>
</tr>
</table>

Actions taken

Since 2016, the Mexican government has succeeded in its efforts to strengthen the legal framework for personal data and privacy protection. In January 2017, the central government adopted the General Law on the Protection of Personal Data handled by Public Entities (Ley General de Protección de Datos Personales en posesión de Sujetos Obligados).[6]

This law further built a basis to increase public trust on personal and private data management by public officials while acting also as an instrument contributing to better governing of the overall data value chain of the Mexican public sector. It reinforced the mandates of other legal instruments such as the 1982 Federal Law on the Responsibilities of Public Servants, the 2005 Guidelines on Personal Data Protection, the 2008 Law on the National Information System, and the 2015 General Law on Transparency and Access to Public Sector Information.

Despite the significant efforts of the government aimed to strengthen the overall framework comprehensiveness, new evidence collected during the OECD peer review to Mexico indicates that some challenges persist in terms of clarity concerning data openness and access for the general public and key actors of the open data ecosystem like journalists. This is for example in regard to the limits of freedom of information and public sector openness requests affecting the publication of, and access to, open government data (e.g. level of data granularity with relation to data protection and personal privacy regulations).

The collaboration of the authority in charge of co-ordinating the open data agenda with the National Institute of Transparency, Access to Information and Personal Data Protection (INAI) remains key in this respect. This, due to the role the INAI has as an active player in terms of public sector data governance - also including its potential role in the development of guidelines to better govern the public sector data value chain (e.g. on data anonymisation).

Overall status of implementation

**Figure 2.3. Implementation of OECD Recommendations:
Governance**

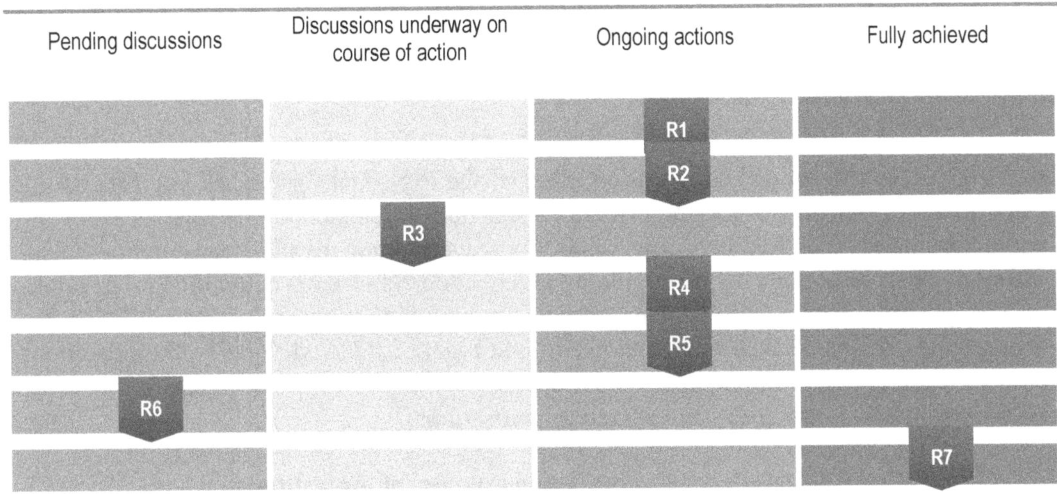

Source: Author.

Towards a demand- and value-driven data disclosure

The 2016 review provided a total of three policy recommendations centring on the relevance of taking further steps to foster a user and demand-driven approach for the publication of open government data. These recommendations aimed to help public sector institutions better identify the needs of data users to prioritise the publication of datasets with high intrinsic value and reuse potential according to the final users, thereby contributing to better focussing efforts inside public sector institutions in relation to data publication.

Recommendation 1

It is necessary to go beyond one-time consultation exercises. *Running regular consultations involving line ministries is crucial to help them connect with different user groups towards the implementation of institutional open data initiatives.*

Status:

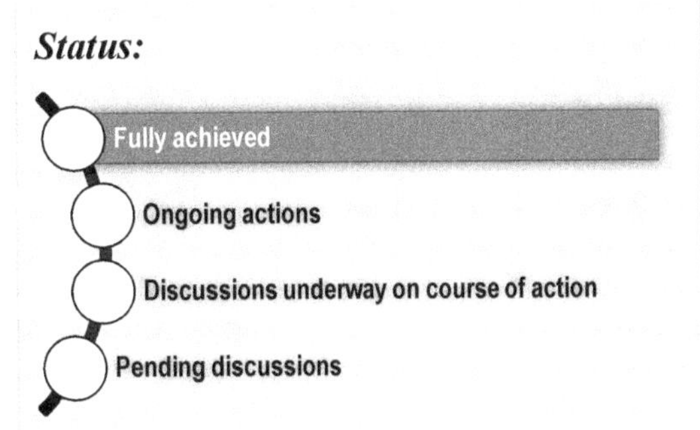

Actions taken

A second exercise led by the General Direction of Open Data was carried out in 2017 to update the Strategic Open Data Infrastructure (IEDA). This exercise drew on the first effort to develop the IEDA that took place in 2015. In this respect, the Mexican government succeeded in developing and implementing a more extensive and exhaustive user-driven version of the IEDA, called MX Open Data Infrastructure[7] (Infraestructura de Datos Abiertos MX, IDMX).

The development of the IDMX consisted of running an online and open survey designed to identify the datasets that users consider have a greater impact on their everyday lives. Participants contributed with their own suggestions and ideas on which datasets to prioritise for release as open data – an approach that made this exercise more open and inclusive in relation to the one adopted in 2015 (when a pre-defined list of datasets was made publicly available for voting).

However, consultation processes aimed to identify data demand remain scarce, and are still highly centralised and run by the Office of the President due to the key role of the General Direction of Open Data in their design and implementation. Results from the survey point to the fact that few institutions have implemented consultations with different open data users to better identify and understand data demand. For instance, only 8 institutions out of 124 report running consultations with representatives from the private sector to learn about their data needs (see Figure 2.4). Additionally, 80 institutions out of 124 report not having run consultations with any user group at all (e.g. private sector, academia, journalists, civil society organisations).[8]

Figure 2.4. Data demand consultation exercises at the institutional level

Data by number of institutions reporting consultation exercises by user group

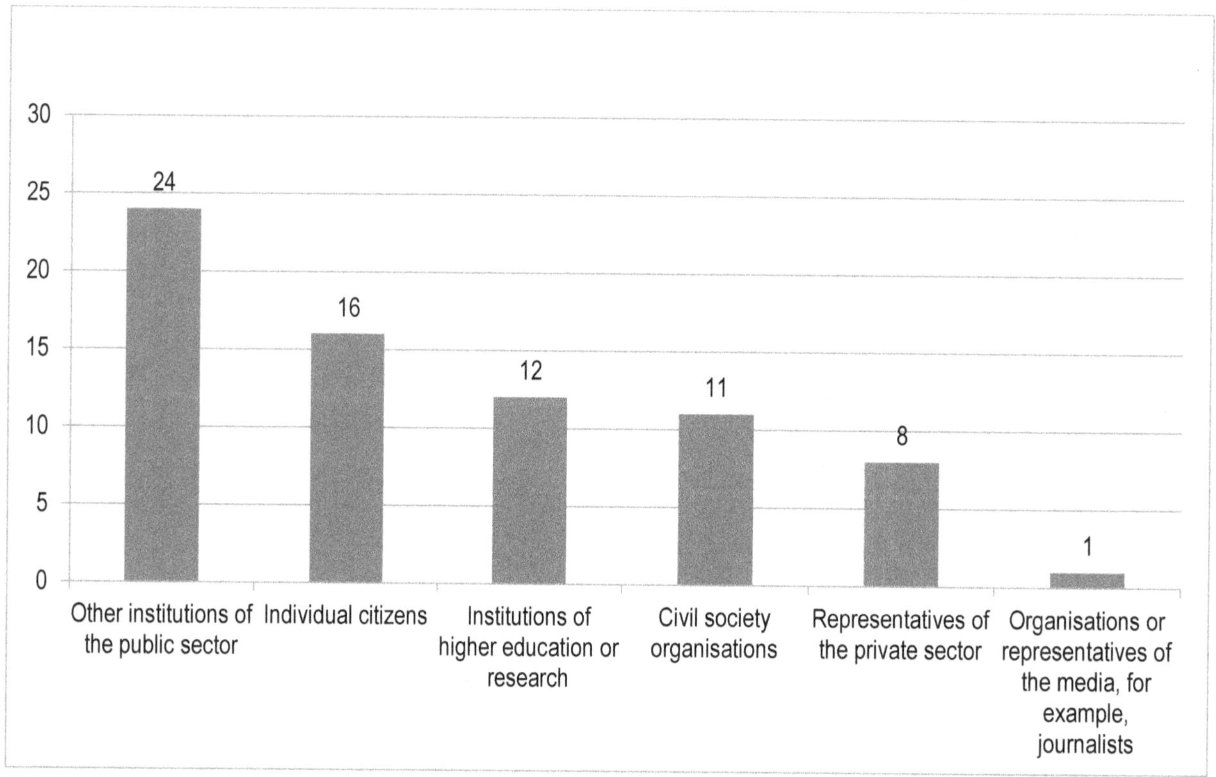

Source: Institutions' responses to OECD (2017a), "Follow-up Survey to the 2016 Open Government Data Review of Mexico", Question 34. ¿Alguna vez su institución ha consultado de manera directa a alguno de estos grupos de usuarios respecto a los datos a los cuales les gustaría tener acceso?

The involvement of public sector institutions in the development of the IDMX infrastructure and other initiatives led by the Office of the President has helped reduce the breach between public sector institutions and data user communities and has also influenced prioritisation efforts for data release, e.g. Retos Públicos or Labora. Nonetheless, the specific definition and implementation of consultation exercises by public sector institutions (in particular, line ministries) remain to be completed as part of the second version of the Open Data Implementation Guide published in December 2017. These consultations will be key to further develop a user- and demand-driven approach for the publication of open government data in Mexico. While the development of the IDMX has been critical to sustaining policy relevance, further consultation processes are required to continuously inform and develop an agile IDMX data infrastructure through policy iteration and feedback loops.

Addressing this implementation gap would require further action especially in light of the new Implementation Guide which includes specific guidance for the implementation of consultation exercises at the institutional level. Efforts and actions in this regard are critical, particularly in consideration of the recognition of data reuse as an essential requirement for public value co-creation (see, for instance, Ubaldi, 2013; OECD, 2017b; OECD, forthcoming).

Recommendation 2

*Establishing **data-request channels** through the central portal is key to identifying data demand while fostering the value of **datos.gob.mx** as a data crowdsourcing platform where users can request and publish open data.*

Status:

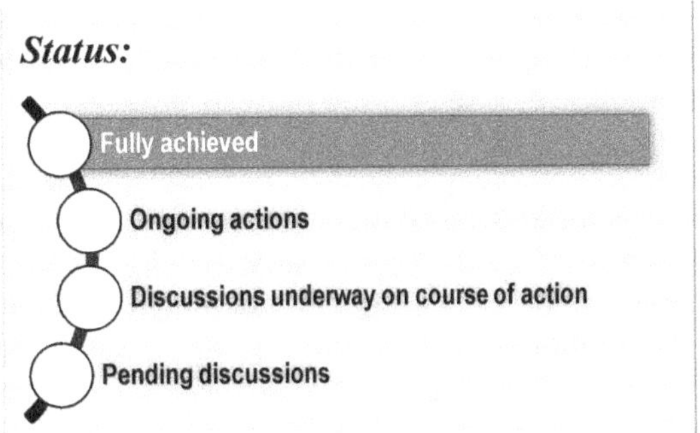

Actions taken

Acknowledging the importance of involving non-government actors in regard to data publication, co-creation and crowdsourcing, the General Direction of Open Data established collaboration with datamx.io - a civic and private open data portal managed by Codeando Mexico (a Mexican civil society organisation [CSO]). The purpose of this collaboration is to design and implement user empowerment mechanisms by connecting the data available on the central OGD portal datos.gob.mx and the aforementioned citizen open data portal. This enhances the contribution of open government data to the overall discoverability and availability of open data. This initiative also contributes to other initiatives implemented by the General Direction of Open Data that aim to democratise the benefits of open data for technical and non-technical user groups (e.g. the inclusion of data visualisation tools in the portal).

In addition, while social media is still the main contact mechanism used by the General Direction of Open Data to respond to data requests, a beta version for direct data requests through the central portal is now available. The new functionality allows users to request data and report issues with specific data resources. There is still room, however, for improvement in regard to the discoverability, user-friendliness and potential of this tool to monitor data causality (e.g. to assess the potential use of data as part of data requests formats).

The role of the Open Data Squad is critical during the entire data request and publication process. Once a data request is submitted by users, it is directed to the Open Data Squad, who assures the validity of the request, and establishes contact with the institution collecting the requested data. The institution then receives and validates the data request and checks the possibility of releasing the data in compliance with the data protection and privacy regulations. If the data is subject to publication, the dataset is included in the Institutional Open Data Plan with a specific date of release. If the data does not exist, or cannot be published, the institution is obliged to inform users on the source and basis of denial in line with the regulations of the 2015 General Law on Transparency.

Recommendation 3

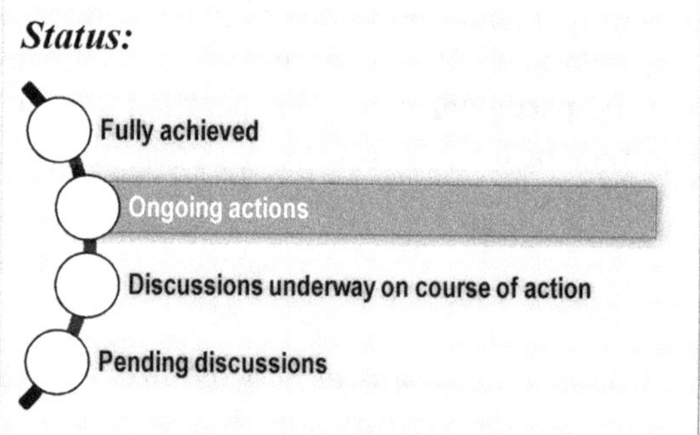

Public institutions disclosing data should acknowledge who their data users are. **Supporting line ministries to connect with their clients** *through* **segment-oriented** *open data marketing and communication strategies is key to further reaching and engaging external stakeholders.*

Actions taken

Reaching and engaging with data users is a priority for the Mexican government. While there is no evidence available on the development of a formal communication strategy since 2016, the Mexican government has taken action to further build capacities inside the public sector in order to reach potential and current users with all levels of knowledge related to the use of open government data (e.g. for instance, through successful initiatives like Labora, the Anticorruption Open Up Guide, Retos México and the IDMX).

From a communication and dissemination perspective, the increased use of online communication tools (such as webinars) by the Office of the President has been pivotal in reaching public officials and data users beyond Mexico City and in building the above-mentioned capacities. Since 2015, the Office of the President has conducted five webinars to develop capacities among public officials (e.g. to create institutional open data plans and develop institutional data catalogues) and produced online content for users on topics such as the data-driven economy and open data for sustainable development. In line with the trend on the increased use of social media channels by governments, the General Direction of Open Data actively promotes its work through Twitter and Facebook.

Overall status of implementation

**Figure 2.5. Implementation of OECD Recommendations:
Demand- and value-driven data publication**

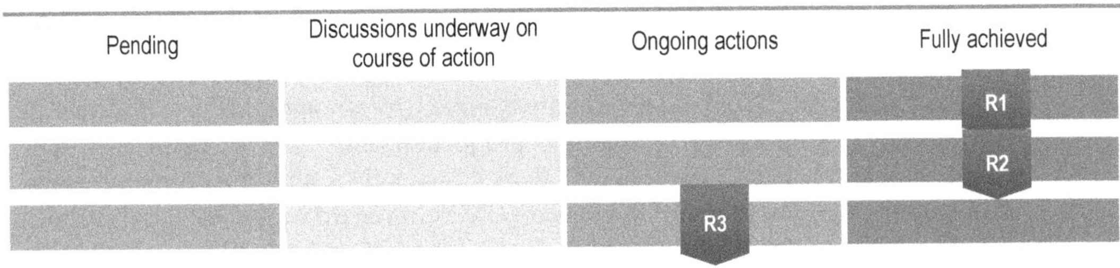

Source: Author.

Building skills across external social user communities and engaging the ecosystem

The relevance of building capacities and skills for data reuse and engagement with key actors of the ecosystem is a core element of open data policies. The growing relevance of civic tech (abbreviation for civic technology) is helping to further build bridges between governments, citizens and civil society. Through the enhanced access and use of digital technologies by civil society organisations and by the general population, civic tech contributes to reinforcing participatory democracy, citizens' participation and engagement and co-creation of good governance value (e.g. public sector accountability, integrity and the fight against corruption), thereby leading to further social empowerment and stronger government-citizen collaboration.

In light of the above, the 2016 review provided four policy recommendations to the Mexican government aiming to advance the creation of good governance and social value in collaboration with key actors of the open data ecosystem in the country.

Recommendations 1 and 2

Providing training and capacity-building activities for society at large and to specific social groups such as journalists is crucial to reinvigorating the ecosystem.

Increase trust in government by partnering with civil society organisations and journalists in order to achieve broader policy goals such as the fight against corruption and strengthening public sector integrity.

Status:

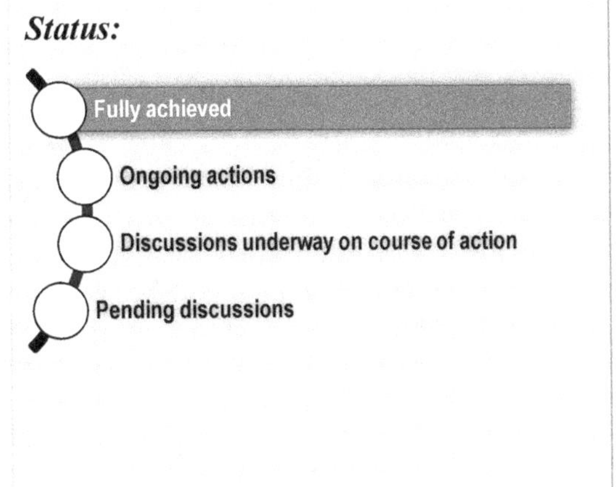

Actions taken

The General Direction of Open Data has sustained and/or launched different initiatives since 2016 in line with the recommendations of the 2016 review, including the following:

- A capacity-building workshop was held in October 2017 in collaboration with the Director-General for Citizen Participation and Violence Prevention at the Ministry of Interior (Secretaria de Gobernación, SEGOB) and the Inter-American Development Bank (IDB). The initiative aimed to strengthen the capacities of civil society organisations to spur the production and reuse of open data. The collaboration consisted in a series of workshops and lectures that aimed to raise awareness among more than 50 Mexican CSOs in regard to the potential of open data and the availability and use of different government tools that can contribute to their work and objectives. These events underscored the role of these organisations as data producers and how the publication of these data through datamx.io (a civic open data portal, as mentioned above) can contribute to enriching data availability, accessibility and reuse. Furthermore, the workshops were used as a consultation forum to assess users' awareness of Mexico's government open data portal, and how the portal is being used to foster the impact of CSOs' work and civic tech.
- Also in October 2017, the Coordination of the National Digital Strategy organised a workshop to develop capacities among users from all sectors in regard to the use of data, including big data, for sustainable development.[9] The workshop was organised in collaboration with the Economic Commission for Latin America and the Caribbean (ECLAC) and Data-Pop Alliance (created by the Harvard Humanitarian Initiative).
- In the context of the implementation of the Open Up Guide on the use of open data for anti-corruption of the International Open Data Charter (ODC), the Mexican government is planning to work with local civil society partners to understand and explore the opportunities and challenges in relation to the publication and reuse of those data taxonomies outlined in the Open Up Guide. The project, implemented in collaboration with Transparency International-Mexico, the Open Contracting Partnership (C5), Open Data for Development (OD4D) and the ODC, has the objective of helping CSOs use the guide as an instrument to spurt public sector accountability and fight corruption in Mexico.
- Mexico sustained its efforts to use the Open Contracting Data Standard (OCDS) as a public procurement transparency and accountability instrument. For instance, to monitor public sector expenditure during the construction of the New International Airport for Mexico City (NAICM), a public-private partnership (PPP) was established as a result of the Telecommunications Shared Network (TSN) (launched in June 2017). The projects add up to a total of 290 contractors and public investments of roughly USD 7.5 billion for the New Airport project, and roughly USD 7 billion for the TSN PPP. The New Airport project's open data is being used by civil society organisations such as Poder and Transparencia Mexicana to monitor the project's procurement processes, contribute to accountability and reduce risks of corruption in the procurement process.
- On 5 January 2017, the Mexican government issued an official regulation to adapt the Federal Procurement System to the OCDS. The regulation, which builds upon the success of the above-mentioned procurement projects, reflects the success of the joint efforts implemented by the Coordination of National Digital Strategy,

and the Ministries of Finance and Public Administration to ensure the interoperability of the Accounting and Budget System (Ministry of Finance) and the Contracting Management System (Compranet). As a result, the Mexican government launched the national open contracting platform www.gob.mx/contratacionesabiertas/ in November 2017.

- In addition, the National Institute for Transparency, Access to Information and Personal Data Protection (INAI) has implemented the OCDS in 88 public procurement procedures. These data are available on the central OGD portal.[10]

Recommendation 3

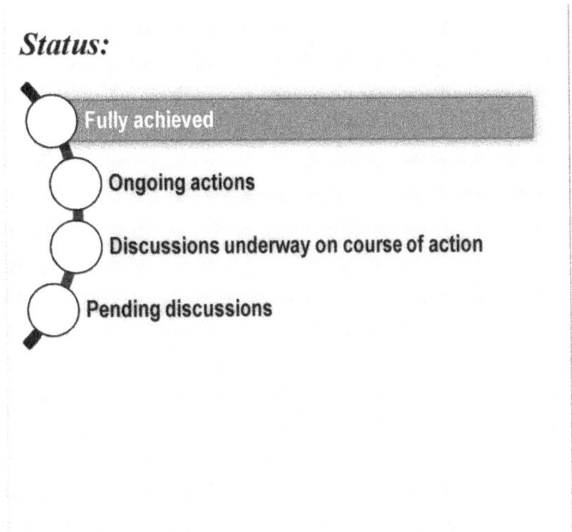

Use and leverage Retos Públicos:

*** as a platform to develop two-way data exchange channels with society in a broad sense** *(i.e. mobile or web-based applications).*

*** to reinforce the capacities** *of* public institutions **to connect with open data communities outside the government.** *Public institutions should be able to implement sector-specific* **multi-stakeholder collaboration exercises,** *in order* **to create greater sector-specific values.**

Actions taken

According to the 2016 review, this recommendation aimed "to increase data crowdsourcing through real-time data [provision] [...] by citizens and other user communities, [in order] to further bring citizens' voice into public decision making, foster citizen-driven public services design and delivery, and increase public accountability."

Retos Públicos enabled greater OGD-enabled multi-stakeholder collaboration centring on specific policy challenges. It also contributed to building greater policy awareness and maturity among public sector institutions in regard to the benefits of open data. As a result, there is a growing trend in regard to the development of sectoral and topic-specific open data initiatives by public sector institutions. For instance:

- The Tax Administration Service (Sistema de Administration Tributaria, SAT) developed the **SAT Más Abierto**[11] **project** as an effort to increase the availability of tax-related statistical information as open data. The publication of these data (based on the Federation Revenue Law for the fiscal year 2017) promotes the monitoring and analysis of fiscal policy in Mexico. The first phase of the initiative includes the publication of open data related to annual tax declarations provided by citizens, companies and other fiscal, legal figures.

- In August 2017, the National Agrarian Registry (Registro Agrario Nacional, RAN) launched the **Public Information Service,**[12] which consists of four online tools that provide data on Mexico's 32 082 *agrarian nuclei* (community-owned rural land, known as *ejido*). These data (available in CSV, Shape and KML formats) covers cadastral registers; the evolution of agrarian nuclei; the list of *ejido* owners; statistics by gender and other indicators of social property.

- **A pilot project to use the Common Alerting Protocol (CAP)** when issuing the AMBER Alert (an early warning alert system for missing children) is currently under development (November 2017). The pilot project is a collaborative effort of the Office of the President, the Office of the General Attorney, and the Special Prosecutor's Office for Crimes of Violence against Women and Human Trafficking (FEVIMTRA). The CAP has also been used as part of data-driven emergency response exercises in Mexico (see Box 2.1).

- **Open data on air quality** is being published on the central OGD portal in an effort to address air pollution in Mexico's largest urban areas. The publication of these data is the result of a joint effort between the Office of the President and the National Institute of Ecology and Climate Change (INECC). These open air quality data provide historical concentrations of air contaminants in Mexico, the location of air monitoring stations across the country, and updates on the levels of contaminants in Mexico's major metropolitan regions such as Monterrey and Guadalajara.

- In light of the results of the energy reform (which brought the end of the state monopoly on oil), and the daily adjustments to petrol prices in force since the first quarter of 2017 (resulting from the dynamics of the global oil market) citizens' access to timely and reliable data on petrol prices has become a priority for the Mexican government. As a result, Mexico's chief data officer (CDO) in collaboration with the Energy Regulatory Commission (CRE), publishes and updates open data on the maximum prices for petrol and diesel on a daily basis. The database provides data for the 90 economic regions in the country in relation to petrol prices, and data on petrol stations' location, management and operation permit (roughly 11 600 at the national level).

- In April 2017, the Mexican president created the **National Council for Sustainable Development Goals (SDGs)** in order to work towards the achievement of the SDGs. The council is comprised of public officials from federal and local governments, and representatives from civil society organisations and the private sector. In line with these efforts, the Coordination of the National Digital Strategy and the INEGI, through the Specialized Technical Committee on Open Data (CTEDA), developed an **open source platform for visualising and consulting indicators on the SDGs** (www.agenda2030.mx). The platform allows users to monitor the progress on the accomplishment of these goals. By December 2017, the platform provided data on more than 80 indicators. The collaboration with the CTEDA is expected to institutionalise the SDGs as part of the Information of National Interest scheme.

In late 2016, the Retos Públicos initiative evolved to Reto México.[13] The objective of Reto México is to act as a multi-stakeholder open innovation platform for the prototyping and co-design of solutions to address policy challenges. The initiative aims to engineer bankable, scalable, replicable projects with a vision of sustainability in the medium term.

While Retos Públicos centred on co-designing solutions for public sector's challenges, Reto México broadened its collaborative approach to private sector needs. Reto México enables private entities to use the online portal retomexico.org to publish project proposals that can benefit from ideas developed by data-driven entrepreneurs. This enables a two-way collaboration platform where the private sector takes an active role in digital innovation and empowers micro and small enterprises to connect with potential clients.

Reto México is now managed by the Ministry of Economy. This addresses the funding sustainability issues that Retos Públicos faced when under the management of the Office of the President (see "Towards a demand- and value-driven data disclosure", Recommendation 2, above). Such an evolution scaled up and contributed to the sustainability of the initiative in the mid and long terms.

**Box 2.1. Data-driven emergency response:
The case of the 19 September 2017 earthquake in Mexico**

On 19 September 2017, Mexico experienced a 7.1 earthquake that caused severe damage in the states of Morelos, Chiapas Estado de México, Guerrero, Oaxaca and Mexico City.

Minutes after the earthquake, the Mexican government, through its National Digital Strategy (EDN) and the National Emergency Committee activated various tools and protocols to respond to the emergency through digital technologies and open data:

- The Coordination of the National Digital Strategy made a public call to the population in order to crowdsource information about damage, shelters and collapses through an open, online database. The exercise resulted in roughly 17 000 data points that were used by public officials and civic organisations to map emergency response initiatives.
- To complement the above-mentioned crowdsourcing exercise, the Government of Mexico released high-value datasets about public Wi-Fi spots, hospitals, structural evaluation of buildings and the list of municipalities declared in "emergency or damage".
- A communication protocol was established between technology companies and the central government in order to multiply the efficiency of the initiatives implemented by different sectors. The objective was to help the population in need and co-ordinate the use and promotion of digital tools such as Google's Person Finder, Alerts and Crisis Map; Waze's data about traffic in Mexico City; Facebook's Safety Check and automated chatbot; Twitter's communication efforts; and Carto's mapping infrastructure.
- Co-ordination with diverse third-sector efforts (e.g. comoayudar.mx and sismomexico.org) contributed to better multi-stakeholder co-ordination for emergency response, better sharing of data through public application programming interfaces (APIs), and the dissemination of information on robust civic initiatives through official channels.
- Drawing upon previous similar efforts no longer in place, Mexico launched an open data-based portal to follow up on the damage and the use of resources for reconstruction. The portal uses the Transparencia Presupuestaria online platform (managed by the Ministry of Finance) – one of the leading public sector openness practices in Mexico.

Currently, the Mexican government is planning to use open data to increase its resilience by working through the National Civil Protection Council to institutionalise a Data and Technology Working Group, high-value open data and establish co-ordination mechanisms with civil society and industry to respond to natural disasters.

Source: Information provided by the Mexican government.

Overall status of implementation

**Figure 2.6. Implementation of OECD Recommendations:
Building skills across external social user communities and engaging the ecosystem**

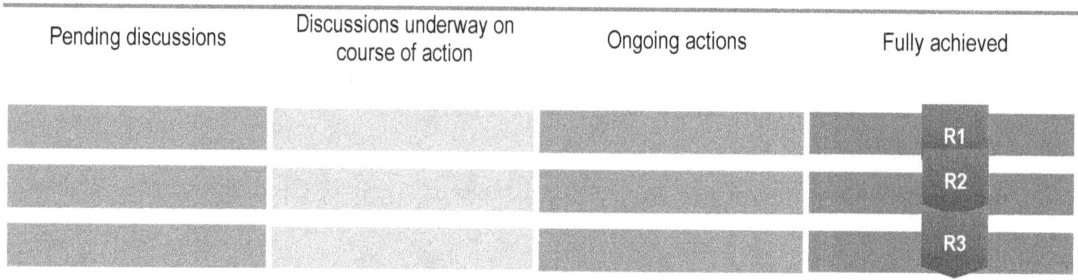

Source: Author.

Open data and the data-driven economy

Results from the 3rd OECD Open Government Data survey (administered across OECD and partner countries in 2016) show that the creation of benefits for the broad economy (e.g. opportunities for the digital economy and data-driven entrepreneurs) is the top policy priority among OECD countries (OECD, 2016). This trend has remained unchanged since the 2nd OECD Open Government Data survey was administered across OECD countries in 2014. Mexico is not the exception to this trend and, amid other efforts that aim to create good governance and social value, the country has equally prioritised the contribution of OGD for the data-driven and digital economy and business innovation in the country.

The 2016 *Open Government Data Review of Mexico* provided a total of three policy recommendations to support the Mexican government on its journey towards the construction of a more mature data-driven ecosystem in the country that favours digital innovation and entrepreneurship.

These recommendations were focused on three priority areas: 1) the publication of valuable and reusable data for the economy; 2) the development of a data-driven business ecosystem; and 3) the development of data skills among for-profit data-driven users.

Recommendations 1 and 2

***Performing consultation exercises aimed at identifying business-oriented data demand could contribute to spurring the value of open government data for businesses.** These consultation exercises would help to establish a business case for the Mexican public sector, thereby convincing the various parts of the administration of the relevance of populating the portal with economically valuable data.*

*Using the current co-operation established with the Ministry of Economy and other bodies, such as the National Institute for Entrepreneurs, it would be beneficial to **develop a data-driven business community.** The Mexican government could consider following the example of Korea and the European Union (EU), which have taken actions to support the development of a data-oriented business community and provide support to OGD-based start-ups.*

Develop partnerships with academic institutions to stimulate data-driven entrepreneurship. This collaboration should aim to invigorate data-driven innovation and create long-term and sustainable economic value through the development of skills from the earlier stages of academic and professional development (e.g. with the development of targeted curricula).

Status:

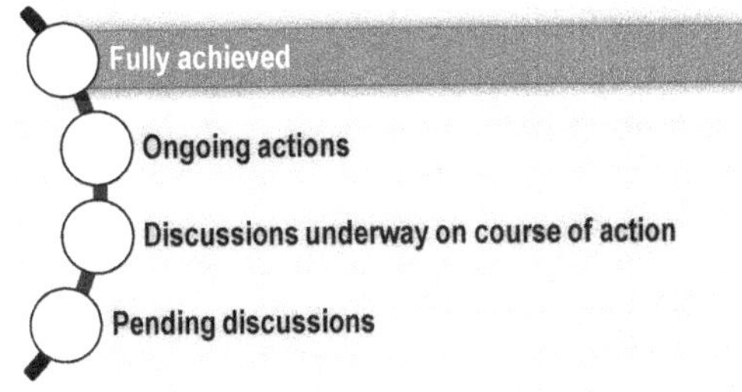

Actions taken

In August 2016, during the launch event of the 2016 review and in line with OECD's recommendations, the Mexican government launched the Labora initiative. The initiative (resulting from a joint effort between the Mexican government, the Open Data Institute [ODI], Demos, and the UK Embassy in Mexico) aimed to create a hub and strengthen the Mexican business ecosystem by providing support to data-driven-based start-ups.

As a business hub, Labora provided a platform where civic and social entrepreneurs could access technical tools and mentorships. The Labora's network empowers participants to establish and scale up their connections with the global start-up ecosystem (e.g. peer networks, high-level advice, investment opportunities) in order to accelerate their impact through digital and data-driven innovation.

The first stage of the initiative aimed to provide a space where entrepreneurs seeking to accelerate the creation of social, civic and economic impact could meet and exchange their practices and views on the context for data-driven business and civic innovation in the country. Among other initiatives, the Mexican government:

- Carried-out the "Train the Trainers" workshop as an effort to build capacities, knowledge and skills on open data among academics and civil society organisations. The workshop aimed to multiply the effect of open data by enabling a cascade out-turn where trainees could replicate and further build their acquired knowledge among their networks. The workshop covered a broad range of topics ranging from pedagogy (e.g. learning models and the approaches of dynamics of knowledge building) and event planning (e.g. workshops, audience-specific training approaches, and the promotion of learning environments).
- Administered a survey across private sector actors involved in Labora to inform and prioritise the publication of OGD that could contribute to economic development as part of the updated version of the Strategic Open Data Infrastructure (now known as IDMX; see "Towards a demand- and value-driven data disclosure", Recommendation 1, above). The survey included a specialised set of questions that explored data publication for economic activities.[14]
- Organised eight roundtables that brought together businesses (using open data as part of their business models) and public officials (responsible for the collection, production and management of high-value datasets). These roundtables were organised as an effort to spur the co-design of evidence-based open data

initiatives aiming to boost economic growth and social impact. Different focus groups were also organised with Mexican data-driven entrepreneurs and potential investors to present the efforts of the Mexican government in regard to open data and discuss the current state of the digital innovation ecosystem in Mexico.[15]

- Partnered with PROMEXICO, a federal agency in charge of promoting business opportunities for Mexican companies worldwide, and organised a conference to present to Mexican and UK start-ups the potential of OGD for business activity. This conference was organised within the context of the UK meets MX week, a shared initiative between Labora and iMobility (an initiative developed by C-Minds - a company providing innovative, digital and social-oriented services for government agencies such as the Office of the President and the DataLab of the Mexico City government).

- Organised a panel within the framework of the 2016 National Entrepreneurs Week (Semana Nacional del Emprendedor) - an event organised by the National Institute for Entrepreneurs (Instituto Nacional del Emprededor, INADEM). The event, attended by roughly 300 people, had the objective of discussing the role of data as an asset for business innovation, and raise awareness among entrepreneurs on the importance and potential of data in innovation and the economic development of Mexico.

In addition:

- The Coordination of the National Digital Strategy - in collaboration with Demos (a US-based CSO) and the Open Data Institute (ODI) held different activities to build further capacities among Mexican public sector institutions. For instance, a workshop was organised to help federal agencies build further data skills among public officials, present the progress of the Open Data Policy, and teach how to generate economic development through the use of data (e.g. by learning and practicing data science basic skills with the support of expert mentors and showing successful case studies). The event had a total of 45 attendees (plus 200 online viewers), including public officials, representatives from international organisations and entrepreneurs interested in developing data-driven project proposals.

- In October 2017, Google Mexico, the Coordination of the National Digital Strategy and the Ministry of Labour established an agreement to standardise the data on employment opportunities published on www.empleo.gob.mx. These data are expected to be published as open data in order to facilitate their reusability through Google's Project Employ Latin America.

- Other areas of work included the organisation of topic-specific training events for public sector institutions in areas such as economic growth, data-driven innovation, the digital economy and sustainable development.

The second stage of Labora (known as Labora 2.0) was launched in 2017 and is expected to kick-off its implementation during 2018 along with the participation of strategic partners such as the UK Embassy in Mexico, C-Minds, the Open Data Institute and FinTech Hub. Labora 2.0 is an effort to multiply the outcomes resulting from the sector-specific generation, publication and reuse of open data for business activity.

Labora 2.0 centres on the emerging and growing Fintech sector in Mexico, thereby aiming to identify what data is needed by private and public sector organisations working with financial technology, the implementation of the Open Banking Data Standard, and building further capacities among this user group. The activities of Labora 2.0 will also aim to work towards the development of an Open Data Standard for the Mexican Banking Community.

The above-mentioned approach is in line with Mexico's recent goal to regulate the Fintech industry in the country. In October 2017, a Fintech Bill was introduced in the Senate by the President of Mexico.[16] The bill (lobbied for over a year with the Congress and expected to pass by the end of 2017) includes specific legal provisions on the obligation of Fintech institutions to develop application programming interfaces (APIs) and make them available for public access so that private and public users can freely and openly collect open financial data from the private sector.

By November 2017, the Mexican government was working to explore the inclusion of open data-related provisions in regional trade agreements of national priority.

Recommendation 3

Develop partnerships with academic institutions to stimulate data-driven entrepreneurship. *This collaboration should aim to invigorate data-driven innovation and create long-term and sustainable economic value through the development of skills from the earlier stages of academic and professional development (e.g. with the development of targeted curricula).*

Status:

Actions taken

Despite the involvement of key academic institutions (such as the Centre for Economics Research and Teaching, CIDE) in relation to specific development of data and digital skills among public officials (see the section below entitled "Towards a data-driven public sector" and the case of the DataLab initiative), or the co-operation between the Ministry of Education and the CEDN for the development of online skill-building initiatives (see "Towards a data-driven public sector", Recommendation 4), there is no evidence of any action taken centred on the long-term development of a skilled base that can contribute to sustainable data-driven innovation and a growing data-driven economy, nor on any current discussion on this topic with the participation of academic institutions.

The above is highly related to policy coherence and the connection of the open data policy to broader policy goals such as educational policy and the development of skills in the context of a digital world.

Overall status of implementation

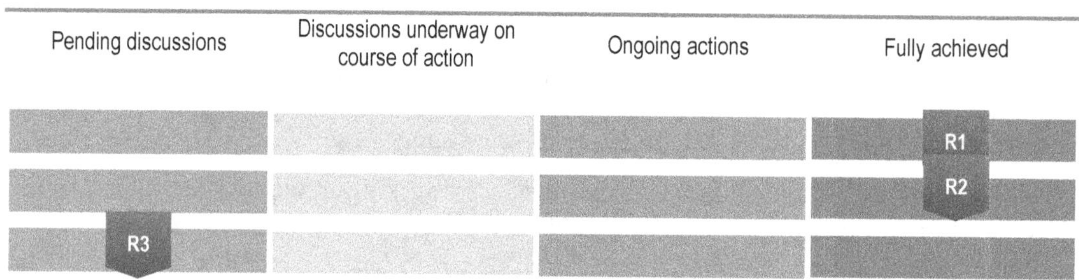

**Figure 2.7. Implementation of OECD Recommendations:
Open data and the data-driven economy**

Source: Author.

Towards a data-driven public sector

The 2016 review underscored the opportunities that digital technologies such as machine-learning and real-time data analytics have brought to public administrations and governments. The review stated the need to move from the strict conception of open government data as an isolated policy to the recognition of its value as an element of a data-driven public sector.

In line with the above, not only open government data should be understood as part of the government data value chain and therefore impacted by the existence of effective data governance models within the public sector, but data itself should be conceived as a strategic asset for data-driven public services design, for strategic foresight and for a more evidence-informed policy making. Accordingly, the 2016 review provided a total of four policy recommendations to help the Mexican government further build capacities to place data at the core of the digital transformation of its public sector. These recommendations mainly focused on designing and implementing data-driven initiatives that take into consideration the role of public sector institutions as data consumers and developing organisational capacities and data skills among public sector institutions towards a data-driven public sector.

Recommendation 1

> ***Involve public officials in the design and implementation of OGD policies, acknowledging their role as data consumers.*** *This should aim to take into account their needs in terms of datasets, software, data quality, skills and organisational support, in order to design policies and programmes that could contribute to more effective inter-institutional data-sharing practices and data interoperability within the framework of open data policies.*

Status:

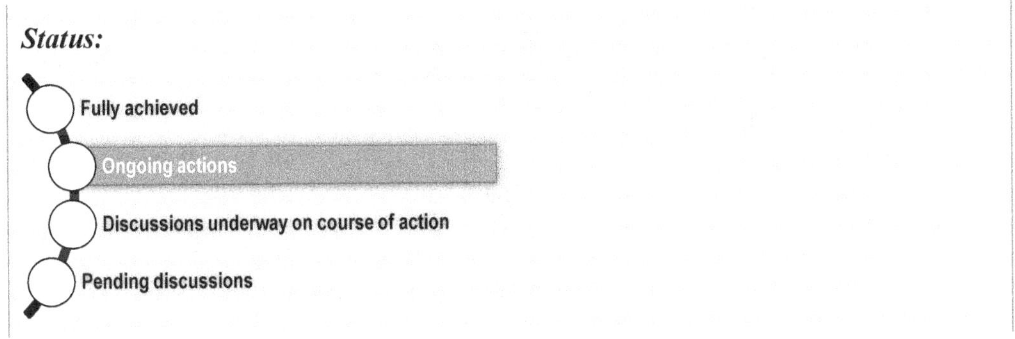

Actions taken

Since 2016, the Government of Mexico has designed and implemented several pilot projects aiming to define a government-wide approach towards the development of data standardisation, sharing and reuse within the public sector within the context of specific OGD initiatives:

- The effective implementation of the Open Contracting Data Standard (OCDS) (see "Building skills across external social user communities and engaging the ecosystem", above) resulted from the definition of a project-specific governance structure involving the Coordination of National Digital Strategy, and the Ministries of Finance (MoF) and Public Administration (SFP). Through this framework, a specific programme was created to develop inter-institutional data sharing practices between the information systems of the MoF (known as SICOP) and those of the SFP (namely, CompraNet). These efforts triggered data interoperability between these two systems in order to comply with the requirements of the Open Contracting Data Standard, which is now being used to feed the National Open Contracting site, www.gob.mx/contratacionesabiertas.

- The OCDS was implemented in Mexico's New Airport and the Telecommunications shared network by specifically analysing data and infrastructure needs in both institutions (see "Building skills across external social user communities and engaging the ecosystem"). These efforts have been documented by the World Bank, and are framed within the context of the Open Contracting Alliance MX and the Open Contracting Partnership (C5). These efforts inform the current implementation of open contracting at the local level through the Open Mexico Network (see "Open data at the local level", below).

- To develop Mexico's National Sustainable Development Platform, agenda2030.mx, the Office of the President worked through INEGI's Specialized Technical Committees on Open Data, and on Sustainable Development, to create data-sharing mechanisms and develop indicators for the 17 SDGs. This mechanism resulted in a multi-stakeholder approach where the General Direction of Open Data supports federal institutions in data standardisation and sharing efforts with the INEGI; which in turn assess the validity of the SDG indicators. These efforts are connected to open data efforts as the CEDN guides public sector institutions for the publication of these data on datos.gob.mx. These data are fed into the site to generate data visualisations and citizen reports.

- Mexico is the first country in the world to implement the Open Data Charter's (ODC) Anticorruption Open Up Guide (AC Guide). It has done so using a four-step work plan that required data interoperability and standardisation efforts:

1. The Open Data Charter, Transparencia Mexicana and Cívica Digital, with the help of the Inter-American Development Bank, carried out inter-agency workshops to identify datasets that could match the ODC's Open Up Guide in the Mexican context.
2. Cívica Digital conducted a standardised evaluation of each dataset according to 15 different variables related to the 6 principles of the ODC.
3. The General Direction of Open Data established an inter-institutional communication mechanism to increase the quality, standardisation, documentation and publication of new and current datasets on the central open data portal.[17]
4. The report and recommendations resulting from the implementation of the ODC AC Guide will inform concrete open data and anti-corruption commitments, including the stewardship of the first Open Data and Anti-Corruption taxonomy list to be developed by the Citizen Participation Committee of the Mexican National Anti-Corruption System.

Yet, despite the development of these initiatives that illustrate the commitment and willingness of the Mexican government to move towards a more mature data ecosystem within the public sector and build data-driven institutions (see Recommendations 2 and 3, below), there is a long path ahead to build data-governance structures that could help streamline data-sharing practices and disrupt legacy frameworks within a public sector made of 300 institutions at the federal level.

Strengthening the former aspects is key to developing stronger building blocks for digital government and the overall digital transformation of the Mexican public sector in connection to open data policies.

Recommendations 2 and 3

Respond to public institutions' needs *and use the Open Data Squads to implement programmes aiming to* ***enhance the institutional capacities for and co-ordination of data analytics throughout the Mexican public administration.*** *Using a larger number of data, from more diverse data sources, and implementing more sophisticated methods of analysis would allow further development of more innovative policies and services.*

In the short term, prioritise key policy sectors for capacity building. *Capacity-building activities could initially be oriented towards increasing the capacities of public institutions working on policy areas or sectors of priority for the Mexican government such as the energy sector. Building these capacities should be included as a* ***strategic component of public sector reforms*** *(thereby contributing to the modernisation and transformation of the energy sector in Mexico) but* ***also as an action line of a more structured open data strategy for the country.***

Status:

Actions taken

The Mexican government launched the DataLab in June 2016. The DataLab was an initiative implemented by the General Direction of Open Data with the main goal of promoting evidence-informed policy making driven by data science and enabled by digital technologies.

The DataLab was a collaborative effort between the Coordination of National Digital Strategy and other federal government agencies, the academia (namely the National Public Policy Lab at the Centre for Economics Research and Teaching [CIDE]), and students and graduates with background on data science, applied mathematics and other related academic areas. It centred on the conception of public sector institutions as data users, therefore aiming to reduce the gap in data expertise within the public sector to foster data-driven policy making.

When created, the DataLab prioritised the administration of a survey across selected public sector institutions including the Ministries of Health, Public Administration and Social Development, the National Institute of Ecology and Climate Change (INECC), and the Mexican Institute for Youth. The survey assessed the state and capabilities of these institutions regarding open data publication and their potential use of data in line with their policy priorities in order to identify how digital technologies (e.g. data analytics) could contribute to their achievement.

As a result of an open call that pooled more than 120 applications, the DataLab brought in six data scientists with a civic background to work as fellows during four months, working on three main projects:

- Representatives from the **Ministry of Health** worked with the fellows and professors at the CIDE to develop a dashboard providing timely information on health performance indicators, and show in practice the value of real-time data for public sector productivity. The cohort also designed advanced data-driven public policy simulations[18] to inform public officials on how timely policy interventions could reduce teenage pregnancy rates in the mid and long terms.
- The **Ministry of Public Administration** worked with the DataLab to explore how data analysis could support the development of an automated system for the prevention, detection and reduction of conflicts of interest, and nepotism in public procurement and civil service appointments.[19]
- The third cohort, which involved the **Ministry of the Interior,** focused on developing a machine-learning algorithm to analyse media coverage on aggressions performed against journalists and human rights defenders in Mexico. The objective was to use natural language analytics to identify risk factors affecting the work of media and human rights defenders.

The DataLab enabled the Mexican government to deliver quick policy wins and raise awareness on the relevance of new technologies and the strategic use of data for government performance. The latter, not only in terms of economic gains but also in terms of social and good governance values connected to policy priorities in the country (e.g. anti-corruption and human rights). As a one-time initiative, the Datalab did not, however, ensure the continuity of capacity-building efforts across the public sector.

This is why, in order to ensure continuity and sustainability, on 1 May 2017, the CEDN created the GobLab as a permanent initiative within the Office of the President. The Goblab is the first formal data and media laboratory for policy making within the Office of the President, working with a multidisciplinary team of data scientists, designers, communicators and human rights experts. Within Goblab, potential solutions for policy issues are engineered based on the mix of digital skills and experimental approaches (e.g. design thinking, user-centric design, machine learning).

On the one hand, the data chapter of the Goblab aims to design data-driven, digital and innovative solutions to the Office of the President and other public sector agencies covering policy areas such as sustainable development, human rights, climate change, anti-corruption and the security agenda. The media chapter, on the other hand, experiments with policy perception, citizen participation and social media in order to provide a stronger evidence base for decision making and policy priorities included on the President's agenda.

As of November 2017, the Goblab was piloting projects in collaboration with the Ministry of Public Administration for the new anti-corruption system, a new food security index to foresee and prevent food shortages in collaboration with the Ministry of Social Development, a new Human Rights Indicators System with the Ministry of the Interior, and the use of open data to follow up on prosecutions cases and missing persons.[20] These projects were being developed with the participation of the United States Agency for International Development (USAID), the Inter-American Development Bank, and academic institutions such as El Colegio de México and Mexico's National Autonomous University (UNAM).

Additional future projects include a pilot project to assess the readiness and potential of data and artificial intelligence for a more efficient, effective and innovative public sector in Mexico. The project (a joint effort of the Office of the President and the UK Embassy in Mexico) will start in early 2018.

The above-mentioned evidence and described projects show the willingness of the Mexican government to foster data-driven public sector innovation with a multi-stakeholder approach relying on collaborative efforts and bringing together a number of public entities, in line with policy and political priorities.

Yet, the strong and central role played by the General Direction of Open Data and the Coordination of National Digital Strategy in regard to project design and implementation, and the still under-developed innovation and data-driven public sector ecosystem, require further capacity building to sustain efforts across the broad public sector. This would contribute to ensuring the continuity and maturity of data-driven public sector innovation efforts in the mid and long terms - beyond the current drive provided by the centre of government - and would achieve systemic change (see Recommendation 4).

Recommendation 4

In the long term, aim to fill existing gaps of core skills and job positions relevant for the sustained development of a data-driven public sector. *This could include foreseeing a skills-development programme across the public sector. The government should assess available data-related knowledge and skills and offer a programme accordingly. Besides ensuring a basic data literacy level for all public servants, efforts should focus on guaranteeing the presence of experts in specific areas, such as data encryption and data quality management.*

Status:

- Fully achieved
- **Ongoing actions**
- Discussions underway on course of action
- Pending discussions

Actions taken

Beyond the efforts and initiatives implemented at the centre of government, the OECD Secretariat found evidence on the design and implementation of initiatives aiming to build data skills among public sector institutions led by other actors, namely:

- From October to December 2017, the Research Centre on Geospatial Information Science (Centro GEO) launched an online course to build capacities on the reuse of geospatial data.[21] The course was available through MexicoX, the eLearning platform of the Ministry of Public Education launched in 2015 in collaboration with the Coordination of the National Digital Strategy.
- The Ministry of Finance (MoF), in collaboration with the Office of the President, launched a massive online open course (MOOC) on the use of open budget data published by the MoF. The MOOC targeted mainly public officials, for it was linked to the development of the evaluation and performance indicators of the Ministry of Finance. Roughly 17 500 people signed up for the course, and roughly 3 900 people completed it.
- The General Direction of Open Data is working (November 2017) on the development of an Open Data Competency Standard with the help and guidance of the National Council for Standardization and Certification of Labour Competencies (Consejo Nacional de Normalización y Certificación de Competencias Laborales, CONOCER). CONOCER, a body within the Ministry of Public Education, is responsible for providing competencies certification, training and evaluation in line with priorities from the private, social and government sectors.
- In 2018, as part of the new Open Data Policy Implementation Guide, the General Direction of Open Data will undertake monthly capacity-building webinars for public institutions.

Overall status of implementation

**Figure 2.8. Implementation of OECD Recommendations:
Towards a data-driven public sector**

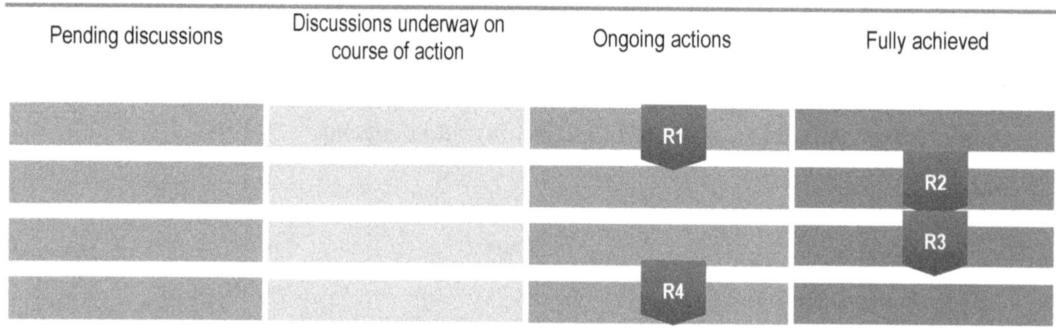

Source: Author.

Open data at the local level

Since its creation in 2015, the Open Mexico Network (Red Mexico Abierto, OMN) enabled co-operation between the central government, and states and municipal governments in Mexico on open-data-related activities. This initiative aimed to establish a nation-wide community of open data practitioners centring on multi-stakeholder collaboration and central-local technical and methodological support.

In light with the above, the 2016 review provided a set of four policy recommendations aiming to increase the relevance of the OMN for the achievement of local, national and supra-national policy goals, while ensuring the multiplying effect of open data initiatives at the central and local levels in Mexico.

Recommendations 1, 2, 3 and 4

Expand the areas of work of the Open Mexico Network drawing upon the business case for open data at the local level in order to increase its relevance for local communities. The OMN should be equally useful to support local governments to develop and implement open data initiatives, contributing to addressing specific local needs, thereby expanding OGD value to various policy areas (e.g. tourism, energy consumption, pollution).

Sustain multi-level collaboration within the framework of the Open Mexico Network in order to keep building a broader vision for open data at the local level in line with the central policy's goals to balance it with local objectives. The work of the OMN will remain of key importance not only to ensure policy coherence but also to further transfer the open data vision from the centre of government to the local level.

The Open Mexico Network could be used as a platform to strengthen horizontal collaboration between local governments in Mexico at the policy implementation level. The OMN could be further leveraged as a platform for horizontal collaboration and support between local governments, focusing its activities on open data matters; and to further connect local governments with the international open data ecosystem.

Co-ordinate with local governments in order to further reach stakeholders at the local level, and work towards greater value co-creation. The active involvement of local stakeholders as enablers of value creation will be strategic to translate Mexico's international commitments on open data into local impact. Sector-specific open data initiatives implemented by social and private organisations at the local level should contribute in a co-ordinated and collaborative fashion to the achievement of the SDGs and the International Open Data Charter.

Status:

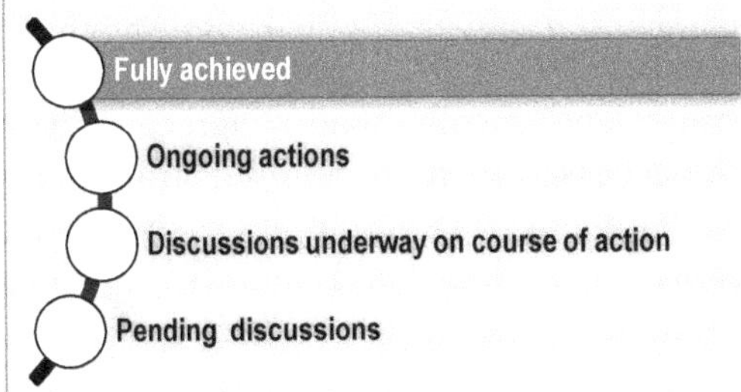

Actions taken

The OECD found evidence of sustained efforts implemented by the Office of the President since 2016 in relation to the development of open data initiatives at the local level, drawing upon the activities of the OMN.

Between 2015 and 2017, the Open Mexico Network promoted kick-start approaches for the development of local open data initiatives, while reducing costs and the duplication of efforts across the country. Building capacities to spur the use of open source technologies and shared resources by local governments played a key role in this respect. This approach was helpful to reduce uncertainty and lack of clarity at the local level, for it ensured the provision of methodological guidance and capacity building among local public servants.

One of the key goals of the Mexican government in earlier stages of the OMN was to develop formal inter-institutional and multi-level co-ordination mechanisms. This required the appointment of institutional contact points within local institutions, thus following a similar approach as applied at the central level. This reduced the risk of fragmented and dispersed central-local communication channels and ensured the efficient flow of tools and support provided by the federal government for the standardisation and publication of open government data.

The growing strategic relevance of this initiative at the political level was reinforced in March 2017 with the signature of a Memorandum of Understanding (MoU) between the Ministry of Public Administration and 31 state governments within the framework of the National Governors' Conference (CONAGO). The MoU drew upon previous efforts that resulted in the integration of 25 municipalities and 9 state governments to the OMN and the acknowledgement of the importance and impact resulting from open data initiatives developed and implemented at the local level.

The MoU aims to level the current disparities in terms of open government data among 32 Mexican states by following a comprehensive approach where all state-level governments (with no exceptions) collaborate, exchange practices and mutually benefit from a shared legal basis (supported by the MoU and the General Freedom of Information Act) for open government data in the country.[22]

Among others, the initiatives below illustrate the results of the OMN:

- The City of Xalapa (State of Veracruz) developed an API to provide real-time data on the location of garbage collection service trucks. The initiative aims to encourage collaboration with the local programming community in order to co-create digital and data-driven solutions that improve the quality of public service delivery.
- In the City of Torreón (State of Coahuila) the publication and analysis of a dataset with car accidents allowed for the identification of road hazards, date/time trends for road accidents, and high-risk streets. These findings enabled the design of a mobility and road safety policy in the city.
- Mexico's National Autonomous University signed a collaboration agreement with the Mexican government to facilitate the access, use, reuse and redistribution of open research data through the central OGD portal, covering topics such as social and economic research, and biodiversity data. The INAI and the National Statistics Office (INEGI) are equally involved in open data efforts at the local level in this regard.
- The development of the National Registration and Cadastral Information Platform by the Ministry of Agrarian, Territorial and Urban Development (SEDATU). The platform comprises the efforts of the national registry in regard to the publication of cadastral registers and agrarian nuclei data (see "Building skills across external social user communities and engaging the ecosystem", Recommendation 3). The platform will integrate information from different government levels regarding various types of property at the local level, therefore favouring territorial development and land-management policies.
- As the result of the effort of the General Direction of Open Data to connect local government to the global open data ecosystem, 18 local governments in Mexico have adopted the International Open Data Charter.

Overall status of implementation

Figure 2.9. Implementation of OECD Recommendations:
Open data at the local level

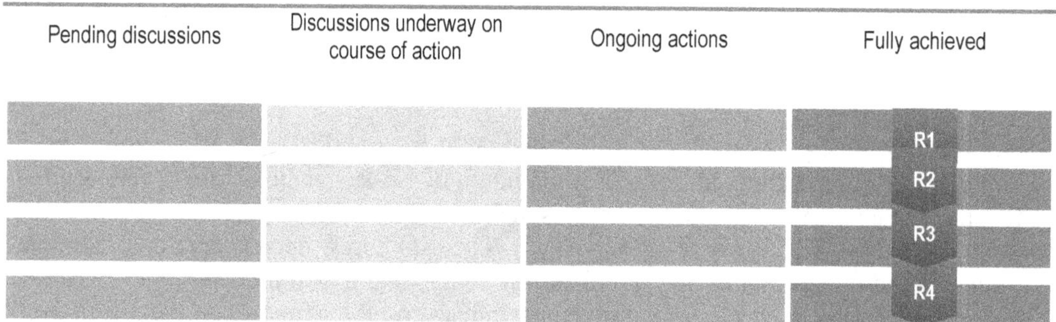

Source: Author.

Notes

1. Institutions' responses to OECD (2017a), "Follow-up Survey to the 2016 Open Government Data Review of Mexico", Question 5. ¿Tiene el gobierno central una estrategia o política enfocada a incrementar la alfabetización sobre la ciencia de datos y datos abiertos dentro de las instituciones públicas y de los funcionarios públicos?

2. Institutions' responses to OECD (2017a), "Follow-up Survey to the 2016 Open Government Data Review of Mexico", Question 6. ¿Qué entiende por el término "datos abiertos gubernamentales"?

3. Information provided by the Mexican government.

4. For more information, see https://github.com/escuadrondatos/datos-abiertos/wiki.

5. Institutions' responses to OECD (2017a), "Follow-up Survey to the 2016 Open Government Data Review of Mexico", Question 8. ¿Cuenta su institución con una estrategia o política pública oficiales (por ejemplo, Iniciativa de Datos Abiertos o Plan de Apertura Institucional) orientadas a un mejor uso de la información recabada o generada por su institución por parte de alguno de los siguientes actorea.

6. For more information: www.diputados.gob.mx/LeyesBiblio/pdf/LGPDPPSO.pdf.

7. For more information, see https://datos.gob.mx/blog/infraestructura-de-datos-abiertos-mx?category=noticias&tag=infraestructura

8. Institutions' responses to OECD (2017a), "Follow-up Survey to the 2016 Open Government Data Review of Mexico", Question 34. ¿Alguna vez su institución ha consultado de manera directa a alguno de estos grupos de usuarios respecto a los datos a los cuales les gustaría tener acceso?

9. For more information see https://datos.gob.mx/blog/taller-datos-economia-digital-y-desarrollo-sostenible?category=proyectos&tag=desarrollo-sostenible.

10. See the central OGD portal at https://datos.gob.mx/busca/organization/inai.

11. For more information, see https://datos.gob.mx/busca/dataset/informes-articulo-decimo-noveno-transitorio-de-la-lif-2017.

12. For more information, see www.gob.mx/ran/prensa/presenta-el-ran-sus-servicios-publicos-de-informacion-del-registro-agrario-nacional and https://datos.gob.mx/busca/organization/ran.

13. For more information, see https://retomexico.org/.

14. For more information, see https://docs.google.com/forms/d/14qG5hDFPVzfjUpRRScM99wSWPzSldhpAhQxsj-ho4q4/edit#responses.

15. For more information, see https://drive.google.com/drive/folders/0B0sdw0fx9FpwUkF1cGlzZmprN3c.

16. For more information, see www.cofemersimir.gob.mx/portales/resumen/43471.

17. See https://datos.gob.mx/busca/group/guia-de-datos-abiertos-anticorrupcion.

18. For more information, visit https://mxabierto.github.io/embarazo_adolescente/fresco/DatalabSaludEA.pdf.

19. For more information, see https://datos.gob.mx/blog/analisis-de-datos-para-prevenir-el-conflicto-de-interes?category=proyectos&tag=seguridad-y-justicia.

20. For more information, see http://104.236.42.158:3000/.

21.	For more information, see http://mx.mexicox.gob.mx/courses/course-v1:CENTROGEO +IAUY17113X+2017_11/about.

22.	For more information, see www.conago.org.mx/reuniones/2017-05-03-jojutla-morelos.

References

Mexican government (1982), "Federal Law of the Responsibilities of Public Servants", http://dof.gob.mx/nota_detalle.php?codigo=4787996&fecha=31/12/1982.

OECD (forthcoming), *Open Government Data Report*, OECD Publishing, Paris.

OECD (2017a), "Follow-up Survey to the 2016 Open Government Data Review of Mexico", OECD, unpublished survey.

OECD (2017b), *Government at a Glance 2017*, OECD Publishing, Paris, http://dx.doi.org/10.1787/gov_glance-2017-en.

OECD (2016), "OECD Open Government Data Survey 3.0", OECD, www.oecd.org/gov/2016-OECD-Survey-on-Open-Government-Data-3.0.pdf.

Ubaldi, B. (2013), "Open Government Data: Towards. Empirical Analysis of Open Government Data Initiatives", *OECD Working Papers on Public Governance*, No. 22, OECD. Publishing, Paris, http://dx.doi.org/10.1787/5k46bj4f03s7-en.

Chapter 3. The way forward:
Towards the sustainability of open government data in Mexico

This chapter presents and discusses the policy recommendations resulting from the analytical framework of the OECD Secretariat in line with OECD benchmarking and best practices across leading OECD countries. The purpose of this chapter is to provide the Mexican government with a set of strategic policy recommendations to support the maturity and sustainability of the open data policy in the short, mid and long terms.

The achievements of the open government data policy in Mexico to date result from the availability of a propitious context comprising different policy elements, including:

- high-level political commitment
- solid political leadership, capacity-building support and technical guidance (which favours increasing institutional buy-in, awareness and skills development across the public sector)
- central policy and clear policy goals (e.g. open data for anti-corruption)
- inter-institutional, horizontal co-ordination (resulting from the instrumental role of the Ministry of Public Administration)
- a flexible and dynamic human resource management at the Office of the President that favours data-driven innovation
- while limited, the availability of financial resources to design, test, mature, co-design and implement policy solutions.

In this context, the Office of the President, with the support of the Ministry of Public Administration, has played a critical and leading role from the centre as:

1. enabler of open data initiatives across the broad public sector (e.g. through the General Direction of Open Data)
2. provider of capacity-building services (through the Open Data Squad)
3. intermediary in charge of ensuring the quality of open government data (through the ADELA Platform managed by the Squad) and making it available through the central portal
4. designer of multi-stakeholder and multi-level collaborative initiatives (e.g. such as Retos Públicos and the Open Mexico Network [OMN]).
5. fundraiser in charge of securing funding to finance its activities, a flexible human resources model, and initiatives.

The above-mentioned conditions and context propelled – in the early stages of open data development in Mexico – the delivery of policy quick wins and the evolution towards a more aware and skilled open data ecosystem within the public sector, capable of designing and implementing open data initiatives coherent with the current high-level policy priorities (e.g. anti-corruption, national development).

Mexico faces the challenge of supporting this momentum in the short term to ensure and contribute to sustainability and maturity in the long term. This would require addressing specific challenges still faced by the Mexican government towards the construction of a data-driven public sector in the country, which requires strategic actions.

Results from the survey show that, according to public sector institutions, the most pressing policy challenges to strengthen and secure continuity and long-term sustainability are related to building capacities within the public sector and across the ecosystem. Institutions need to be provided with the incentives and the capabilities to exploit the potential of data at the institutional and sectoral level. It is thus necessary for the federal government to emphasise the critical importance of data reuse for co-creation of value by institutions and the open data ecosystem at large. Moving towards this direction and prioritising efforts in this sense, is essential to move from a situation where initiatives are engaging other actors - particularly those across the public sector - are still primarily driven by the Office of the President to a context characterised by more "bottom-up" initiatives genuinely emerging from the interest of the different actors.

Figure 3.1. Priority areas of work for policy continuity and sustainability

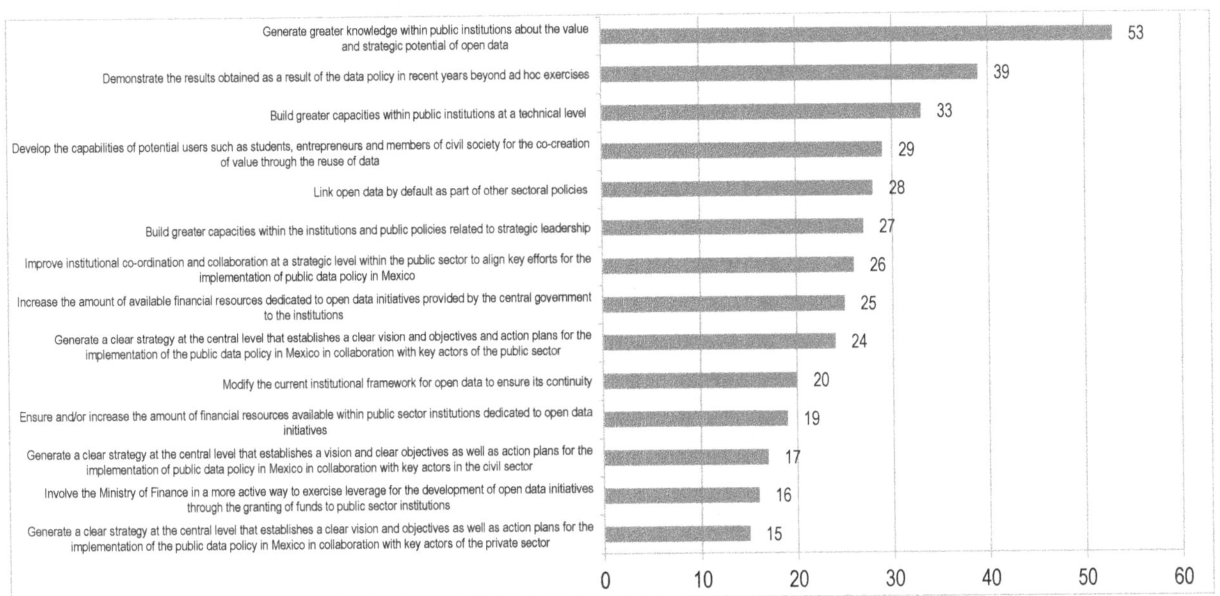

Source: Institutions' responses to OECD (2017a), "Follow-up Survey to the 2016 Open Government Data Review of Mexico", Question 47.¿Qué acciones se pueden llevar a cabo actualmente para fortalecer y dar continuidad a la Política de Datos Abiertos?. Number of public sector institutions selecting "1.0: Urgent/priority actions".

Evidence demonstrates that the five most considered required actions to sustain and strengthen open data policy concern the greater reuse of open government data (OGD) by all potential users (i.e. entrepreneurs, students, members of the civil society, public institutions). For instance, 53 out of the responding 124 institutions[1] consider that there is an urgent need to generate greater knowledge within public institutions about the value and strategic potential of open data. Yet, ensuring the implementation of actions for capacity building is conditioned on the sustained availability of a propitious governance context in charge of defining, leading and co-ordinating these activities. The latter becomes highly relevant in the Mexican context due to the still maturing public sector approach for open government data in the country.

The following sections present a set of strategic policy recommendations that aim to support the Mexican government in advancing and sustaining successful implementation of the open data policy. These recommendations are presented as short-term (<1 year), mid-term (1-2 years), and long-term (>2 years). Annex A presents a summary of these recommendations along a proposed timeline.

Governance

Evidence collected during the OECD peer review mission to Mexico shows that there is a need to sustain the high-level political support for open government data in order to promote policy continuity and sustainable results across government administrations.

Institutional governance

As shown in Chapter 2. , in general, the leadership and advancements in terms of policy implementation in Mexico are clear. Nonetheless, building on the recognition of the relevance of the open government data policy as a core area for a more innovative and performing public sector, it is critical to secure its permanence and continuity, which is highly conditioned by the existence of a sound institutional governance model - sustainable and resilient to political cycles (i.e. changing political agendas) - by the availability (or lack) of a constant flow of financial resources supporting policy co-ordination at the centre of government and government-wide implementation.

The Mexican General Director of the Open Data (*de jure*) acts as the effective chief open government data officer in the country, and when needed, also operates as the chief data officer (CDO) (*de facto*) in collaboration with the Ministry of Public Administration. However, the permanent nature of this position and function, and its subsequent resilience in the long term and across political transitions is unclear.

Evidence from the OECD Open Government Data Survey 3.0 shows that the location of the authority responsible for formulating the OGD strategy/policy within the central executive office contributes to effective policy co-ordination across the administration, and secures high-level political leverage and recognition broadly among public institutions. For instance, responsibilities in the United Kingdom to lead the co-ordination of the open data policy lie with the Government Digital Service (GDS), a body within the Cabinet Office and governed by the Ministerial Group on Government Digital Technology. This location enables GDS to better steer and co-ordinate the digital transformation of the public sector (including open data) and to ensure systemic change across public sector departments and agencies. In France, Etalab (the French Task Force for Open Data) is part of the Inter-ministerial Directorate of Digital and Information System and Communication of the State, which falls under the Office of the Prime Minister, hence giving this body strong leverage to enforce the government's decisions and horizontal agendas across institutions. The different executive decrees that have been issued in France, noticeably the recent decrees in November 2017,[2] clearly define the responsibilities of Etalab and its structure.

Evidence also confirms the importance not only of the location but also of the permanent nature of the institutional set-up, for the long-term sustainability and resilience of the governance of open data. In this sense, requirements include a clear source and basis for the mandate of the bodies and specific function in charge of the open data policy and agenda so as to assert their authority, sustainability and legitimacy with relation to other public sector institutions. In Korea, the Open Data Law stands as the archetype to a clear and solid source of the mandate for the National Information Society Agency (NIA). Article 13 of the Korean Open Data law specifically mandates the NIA the responsibility to "provide support for promoting the provision and use of public data" (Government of the Republic of Korea, 2016) (see Figure 3.2).

Given the horizontal nature of the OGD policy, in Mexico, the authority leading the development of the OGD policy, as well as the co-ordination of its implementation, needs to be sufficiently empowered. This implies having a clear and strong mandate based on a solid legal basis, an institutional set-up granting strong political support and leadership, the possibility of counting on the necessary policy levers for sustained, and effective, co-ordination and implementation.

Figure 3.2. Models of institutional governance across selected OECD countries

France➔ Etalab

- Under the office of the Prime Minister
- Executive decrees are the source of its mandate
- Budget allocation provided by central government
- Co-ordinates the open data policy and data reuse

United Kingdom➔ Government Digital Service (GDS)

- Under the Cabinet Office
- The Government Transformation Strategy is the source of the mandate
- Budget allocation provided by the central government
- Leads the digital transformation in the government

Korea➔ National Information Society Agency (NIA)

- Under the Ministry of Interior and the Ministry of Science and ICT
- Law is the source of its mandate
- Budget allocation provided by central government
- Leads the digital transformation in the government

Source: OECD (forthcoming), *Open Government Data Report*, OECD Publishing, Paris, with data from OECD (2016a), "OECD Open Government Data Survey 3.0", OECD, www.oecd.org/gov/2016-OECD-Survey-on-Open-Government-Data-3.0.pdf.

Results from the survey that was administered for the purpose of this project (see Figure 3.3) indicate that, according to the responses provided by public sector institutions, the following elements would be preconditions for policy success in terms of institutional governance in Mexico:

- **Availability of a clear function/role**: There needs to be a figure with sufficient power and levers to compel all dependencies of the Federal Public Administration (APF) to implement all elements of the open government data policy. In this line, the institutionalisation of such function as a permanent role in the Mexican administration and its location within the Office of the President, or within a body directly accountable to it, would provide the strongest level of authority to lead and co-ordinate with the entire APF and contribute to effective policy implementation.
- **Autonomy of the function/role:** The figure and its supporting institutional environment needs to be autonomous and disentangled from the political cycle if it is to avoid conflict of interest and remain: 1) objective in the design of open data policies; and 2) dynamic in the operationalisation, co-ordination and implementation of the open data policy across the broad public sector. Sound governance structures shield the work of the function/authority in charge of formulating and implementing the open data policy from political cycles (e.g. through financial autonomy), potentially undermining long-term continuity of initiatives (OECD, 2016b). The function/authority in charge of formulating the open government data policy must have the freedom of self-determination in order to create and implement efficient open data policies that are not conditioned by specific political priorities, but that contribute to policy agendas of national interest.
- **Specialised institutional environment:** Given the recognition of the value of government data and open data as a strategic element of the digital transformation of the public sector, efforts dedicated to ensure follow-up with institutions on the

implementation of open data policies would benefit from stronger institutional linkages with the entity in charge of the digital transformation of the public sector. This would enable the Mexican government to strengthen the reuse of open data (and data) within and outside the public sector as part of its digital government initiatives. This could be secured, for instance, by establishing a specialised institution focusing on all aspects related to digital government and to the digital transformation of the public sector (e.g. GDS in the United Kingdom, NIA in Korea, the Digital Italy Agency/AgID in Italy), that would include responsibilities on open government data to capitalise efforts on open data reuse as an asset for the creation of a data-driven public sector (e.g. Agency for Digital Government).

Figure 3.3. Mexico's public sector institutions' views on the ideal model of institutional governance for a sustainable open data policy

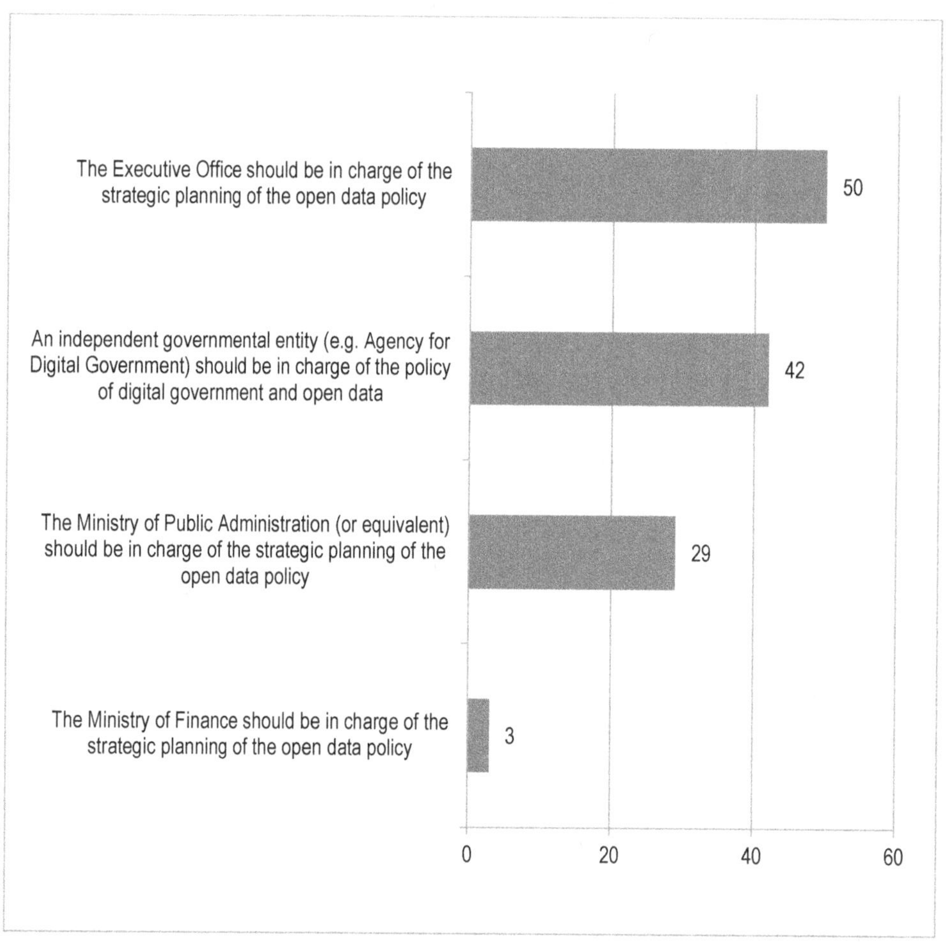

Source: Institutions' responses to OECD (2017a), "Follow-up Survey to the 2016 Open Government Data Review of Mexico", Question 46a. En su opinión, ¿Cuál sería el modelo ideal de gobernanza institucional para la sustentabilidad Política de Datos Abiertos en México?

All these different elements are identified as essential to create a sound and effective institutional governance framework that can contribute to the long-term sustainability of the effective implementation of the open data policy in Mexico. Power (based on clear legitimacy drawing on solid political, financial and legal basis), specialised knowledge and autonomy are all interdependent elements to consider when establishing the governance framework of the open data policy. Thus, an important reinforcement of the current governance framework would support the evolution towards a more mature open data policy, therefore contributing to its long-term success and continuity.

The government could consider either creating an independent function and supporting institutional structure responsible for open data or at least reconsider the mandate, responsibilities and structure of the existing General Direction of Open Data to provide it with the necessary power, resources and support. Nonetheless, it will be essential for the location of the function and the basis of its mandate to reconcile all the different elements mentioned previously, e.g. co-ordination powers need to be reconciled with independence from political cycles, and the need for specialisation.

Chief data officer

The experience from OECD countries shows that clear and strong leadership is an essential feature to lead public sector data governance, promote greater levels of data availability, secure data accessibility, and encourage the government's support for open government data reuse.

Evidence demonstrates that the top five countries in the 2017 OURdata Index (France, Japan, Korea, Mexico and the United Kingdom) have prioritised the establishment of the official position/function of a chief data officer (or a position with these responsibilities) within their central/federal government (see Figure 3.4). For instance, in France, the position of chief data officer (*Administrateur général des données*, AGD) was created as a result of the Prime Minister's Official Decree No. 2014-1050 on 16 September 2014 (OECD, 2016a). In the United Kingdom, the 2017-20 Government Transformation Strategy clearly states the relevance of the role of the CDO for the overall digital transformation of the public sector.[3] This evidence supports the fact that chief data officers are an important asset in terms of leadership and systemic policy co-ordination.

Chief data officers co-ordinate the different administrative actions covering the whole government data value chain of the public sector (e.g. the creation of open data catalogues) and monitor the implementation of central policy and technical guidelines supporting data governance (e.g. technical norms for data interoperability or publication).

Regarding the adequate empowerment of the chief data officer, evidence suggests that the location within the government of such an authority is essential. With the exception of Korea and Colombia, all countries for which the CDO is within the central/federal executive/cabinet office tend to perform much better. Leadership, co-ordination and guidance through the availability of a CDO stands as a vehicle for the fulfilment of data governance and open data strategies, necessary for a data-driven public sector. CDOs have a strategic vision of data governance, are adequately empowered to efficiently co-ordinate central bodies towards synchronised and well-structured policy goals (including open government data) and can count on soft and/or hard policy levers.

Figure 3.4. Availability of a chief data officer in the central/federal government across OECD countries and partners

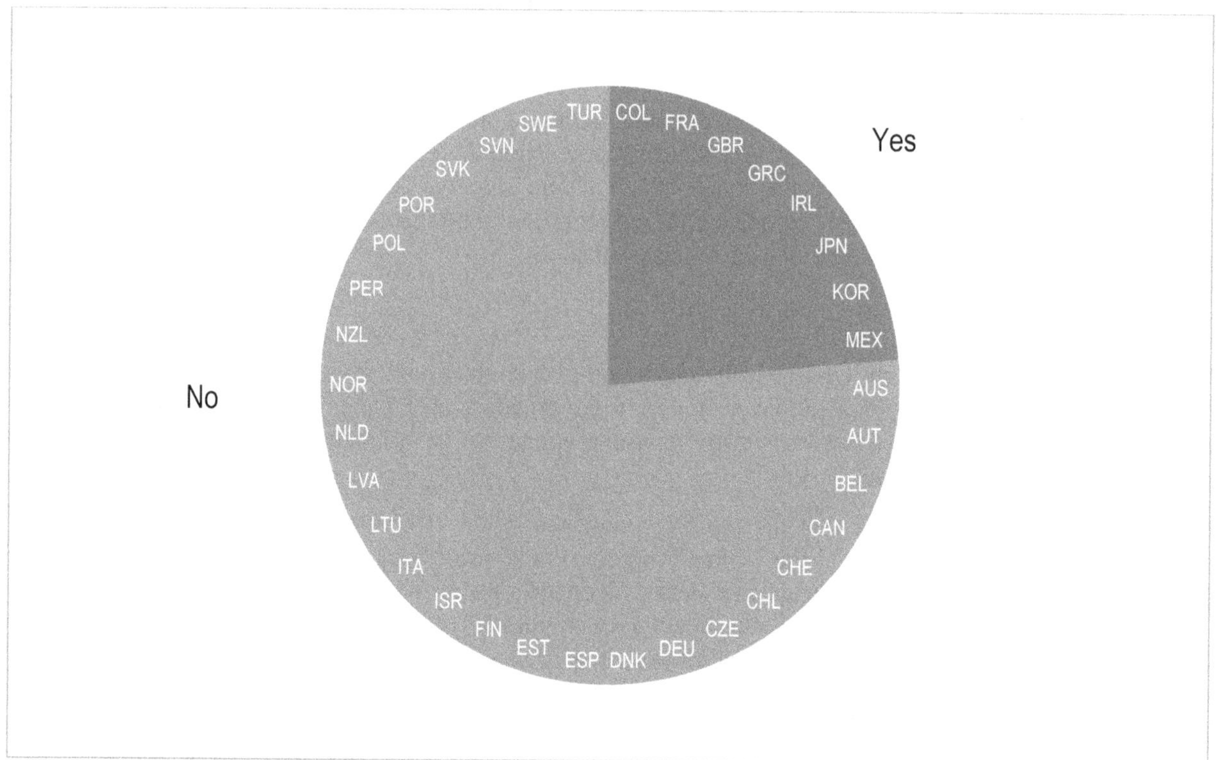

Source: OECD (forthcoming), *Open Government Data Report*, OECD Publishing, Paris, with data from OECD (2016a), "OECD Open Government Data Survey 3.0", OECD, www.oecd.org/gov/2016-OECD-Survey-on-Open-Government-Data-3.0.pdf.

In light of the above, the Mexican government may consider implementing the following policy recommendations in the mid term:

- Institutionalise and formalise the positions of a chief data officer and chief digital transformation officer within the Office of the President. Strategic policy definition and leadership roles should be maintained within the Office of the President in order to grant political support to the definition and co-ordination of the overall implementation of the open data and innovation policies in the country in line with the strategic priorities defined by the overall digital agenda and coherent with the digital government strategy (medium-term action). The civil servants responsible for these roles should at least have a level of undersecretary to be successful.
- Consider the creation of a digitalisation agency in charge of co-ordinating the *digital agenda* in the country, including digital government, open data and public sector innovation policies:
  - o This would further contribute to securing the alignment of different policy efforts, funding, capture synergies among relevant policies, facilitate economies of scale and avoid duplication and fragmentation of endeavours (long-term action to secure – overall - the sustained contribution of the actions in these cross-cutting policy areas to broader policy goals [e.g. National Development Agenda and the Sustainable Development Goals]).

o Sustaining the close collaboration between a newly established institution/agency and the Office of the President will remain critical to ensuring the political support and leverage, the high-level visibility of the open data policy, and a risk-based accountability mechanism to ensure control and monitoring from the centre of government.

Policy funding

As discussed in Chapter 2. , the current funding model for the open data policy in Mexico is not sustainable in the long term, and subsequently, resources (both human and financial) supporting effective implementation, are not secured. This context limits the possibility to use financial levers to spur the development of open data initiatives across the public sector. Indeed, Mexico stands as the only OECD country reporting irregular OGD policy funding from other public sector institutions (see Table 3.1).

A solid and well-defined funding model facilitates designing, implementing and sustaining different open data initiatives in the long term. Sustainable and secure funding is critical for policy continuity and maturity, as a firm financial basis provides the institution with room for manoeuvre and flexibility to implement its open data strategy and plans efficiently and effectively – coupled with the parallel appropriate accountability, monitoring and evaluation mechanisms in place (see "Monitoring actions and delivering results to support policy sustainability", below).

Additionally, clear and sustainable funding guarantees protection from the influences of political cycles, thereby acting as a lever to promote open data policies sustainability and continuity. Thus, the funding model must be designed with the intent of eliminating all possible constraints to policy implementation and sustainability in the long run (see Box 3.1).

Within ministries and public institutions, most entities (108 out of 111 institutions[4]) use funds from their general budget to implement their institutional open data initiatives (mainly focused on opening up OGD in line with central guidelines). As a result, in most cases, there is no specific budget allocated to promote and capitalise on the value of open government data broadly.

Together, the absence of a concrete vision regarding open government data at the institutional level, the lack of financial resources and of data stewardship across institutions (see "The role of public sector institutions: Data stewardship", above) propels a focus on the publication of open government data rather than on its strategic reuse (within institutions and across the open data ecosystem). Institutions have focused on opening up the data with the resources at hand, but not on exploiting its value for specific purposes/institutional objectives, which would have benefited from either the availability of a dedicated institutional budget or further financial support provided by the central co-ordinating agency specifically for OGD.

In light of the still-maturing public sector open data ecosystem in Mexico, the availability of dedicated financial resources at the institutional level and/or funding available for the co-ordinating entity to use as a policy lever would act as a critical tool to further build institutional capacities, strengthen the institutions' understanding of the strategic role of open data, and design and implement multi-stakeholder open data initiatives.

Table 3.1. OGD policy-funding models across OECD countries and partners

	Government assigns its own line of financing to the OGD strategy/policy	Funding from other public sector institutions to fund the OGD policy/strategy but funding is not regular	Government provides funding to other public sector institutions to implement their OGD initiatives	Each public sector institutions finances its specific OGD initiatives	Funding from the private sector	Funding from the civil society	Grants from international organisation	Royalties for some data	Advertisement	EU structural funds
Australia	●	○	○	●	○	○	○	○	○	○
Austria	○	○	○	●	○	○	○	○	○	○
Belgium	○	○	○	●	○	○	○	○	○	○
Canada	●	○	○	●	○	○	○	○	○	○
Chile	●	○	○	●	○	○	○	○	○	○
Czech Republic	○	○	○	○	●	●	○	○	○	●
Denmark	○	○	○	○	○	○	○	○	○	○
Estonia	●	○	●	●	○	○	○	○	○	●
Finland	○	○	●	●	○	○	○	○	○	●
France	●	○	○	○	○	○	○	○	○	○
Germany	●	○	○	●	○	○	○	○	○	○
Greece	○	○	○	○	○	○	○	○	○	○
Ireland	●	○	○	●	○	○	○	○	○	○
Israel	●	○	●	●	○	○	○	○	○	○
Italy	●	○	○	●	○	○	○	○	○	●
Japan	●	○	●	●	○	○	○	○	○	○
Korea	●	○	●	●	○	○	○	○	○	○
Latvia	○	○	○	○	○	○	○	○	○	●
Mexico	○	●	○	○	○	○	○	○	○	○
Netherlands	○	○	○	●	○	○	○	○	○	○
New Zealand	●	○	○	○	○	○	○	○	○	○
Norway	●	○	○	●	○	○	○	●	○	○
Poland	○	○	○	●	○	○	○	○	○	●
Portugal	○	○	○	●	○	○	○	○	○	●
Slovak Republic	○	○	●	○	○	○	○	○	○	●
Slovenia	●	○	○	●	○	○	○	○	○	●
Spain	●	○	○	●	○	○	○	○	○	○
Sweden	○	○	○	●	○	○	○	○	○	○
Switzerland	●	○	○	●	○	○	○	○	○	○
Turkey	●	○	○	○	○	○	○	○	○	○
United Kingdom	○	○	○	●	○	○	○	○	○	○

● Yes
○ No

Colombia	●									
Lithuania	●			●						●
Peru	●			●						

Source: OECD (forthcoming), *Open Government Data Report*, OECD Publishing, Paris, with data from OECD (2016a), "OECD Open Government Data Survey 3.0", OECD, www.oecd.org/gov/2016-OECD-Survey-on-Open-Government-Data-3.0.pdf, Question 22. Countries providing a response to the question: Please indicate how OGD is funded in your country.

Box 3.1. Funding OGD policies across selected OECD countries

Across OECD countries, the type of financing provided to the authority co-ordinating the OGD policy also plays an important role:

- In the case of Portugal for example, the financial autonomy of the Agency for Administrative Modernisation (AMA) (a body within the Presidency of the Council of Ministers) constitutes an interesting approach to protect decisions and investments on OGD from influences from the political cycle, and secure funding to carry out its responsibilities and secure continuity of initiatives. AMA also uses EU Structural Funds as levers to ensure the inclusion of open data as part of public sector institutions application for funding.
- In the United Kingdom, the funds allocated to the GDS, with the provision of GBP 450 million over 2015 to 2019, constitute a solid financial basis to enable GDS to implement its different programmes for digital transformation (HM Treasury, 2015: 70).
- In France, the Secretariat-General for Government Modernisation's (SGMAP) received in 2016 funds of about EUR 41 million, of which EUR 2.5 million was allocated to the publication and use of open government data. Etalab uses this budget to develop different open data initiatives, including the development and management of the central open government data portal, and exploit the potential value of OGD through data science in order to promote a data-driven public sector (Office of the Prime Minister, 2015: 67-68).

Source: OECD (forthcoming), *Open Government Data Report*, OECD Publishing, Paris.

In light of the above, the Mexican government may consider implementing the following policy recommendations in the mid and long terms:

- In line with other OECD countries, consider the creation of a dedicated fund on open data for the entity/authority/function in charge of defining the open data policy and co-ordinate its implementation. This would be a policy lever providing incentives and supporting institutions' activities on open data:
  - The creation of a dedicated fund covering the implementation of the OGD policy would also contribute to the overall implementation and success of the National Development Plan, the National Digital Strategy, and the Programme for a Closer and Modern Government.
  - Given the Mexican context, the above-mentioned dedicated fund could be managed by the newly created agency/institution in charge of the digital agenda or could be assigned to the Ministry of Public Administration, similarly to what happens in the case of digital government.
- Increase the involvement of the Ministry of Finance (MoF) in terms of policy implementation. Closer collaboration between the Office of the President, the Ministry of Public Administration, and the MoF can help embed open data as an element of broader policies and link discussions on the relevant funding to the overall budget cycle in the country:

- o Applications for federal funding (e.g. through the development of business cases for digital projects) for specific digitalisation and digital government projects can be used to enforce the development of open data initiatives as part of these projects. The advisory role of the Ministry of Public Administration and the Office of the President (in terms of granting funds for information and communication technology [ICT] project proposals in line with their relevance and contribution to the open data policy) can contribute to this purpose when linked to budget allocation.
- Create/envisage a specific budget line in the institutional budget dedicated to the overall digitalisation of the public sector, including the sustainability of the open data policy.

Legal framework

Traditionally, there is strong tendency across OECD countries for drawing upon transparency and freedom of information acts as the legal basis for open government data (Ubaldi, 2013). This rationale explains why open government data is often conceived as an evolution of access to public sector information and transparency policies. Even though they are strictly linked, this approach has in many circumstances led to strong transparency-driven approaches affecting the overall dynamics and understanding of open government data.

The work of the OECD in specific regions has for example found evidence on how the aforementioned context and approach have led to governments' passive/reactive approaches to open government data driven by public sector transparency arguments rather than building on the understanding that proactive release of data is an essential precondition for public value creation, beyond transparency. A strong focus on transparency, though essential to sustain efforts meant to strengthen overall public sector integrity and accountability, can limit the proactive release of open government data and the necessary engagement of the relevant actors in the ecosystem in data reuse for value creation.

Furthermore, the experience of some OECD countries shows how changes in the central administration and political cycles could bring policy uncertainty, in particular when the OGD policy emanates from legal instruments issued by the Executive (which can be abolished by the subsequent administration). The OECD analysis of different legal instruments specific to both public sector digitisation or open government data demonstrates the importance of how sound legal and regulatory framework can foster data-driven and digital public sectors.

Some OECD countries have taken action in this respect by developing specific legal instruments devoted to public sector digitalisation or, in more specific cases, open government data to secure the establishment of solid legal basis for open data policy, as a key requirement for its long-term sustainability and continuity, beyond Executive Decrees or Freedom of Information acts (see Table 3.2). For instance, the 2013 Act on the Promotion, Provision and Use of Public Data in Korea, the 2016 Digital Law (Loi Numerique) in France, and the 2017 Law for the Promotion of Electronic Government (E-Government Law) in Germany. In the United States, the Open, Public, Electronic and Necessary (OPEN) Government Data Act was (re)introduced to the US Congress in October 2017 as part of the Foundations for Evidence-Based Policymaking Act.

Table 3.2. Key legal and regulatory instruments on OGD across selected OECD countries

	Argentina[1]	Brazil[2]	France[3]	Germany[4]	Korea[5]	Mexico[6]	Peru[7]	United States[8]
Requires explicitly the publication of open data in a machine-readable format and in open format with their associated metadata	■	■	○	○	○	■	■	●
Demands the publication and update of an open data catalogue for all institutions	■	■	●	○	●	■	▲	●
Provides a taxonomy of datasets to be published in priority	■	■	●	○	○	○	○	○
Mandates a national chief data officer	○	■	■	○	●	○	■	○
Mandates institutional chief data officers within all public sector institutions	○	○	○	○	●	○	○	●
Mandates the appointment of public officials in charge of data publication	○	■	▲	○	●	▲	■	●
Requires the publication of open data plans by public sector institutions	○	■	●	○	●	▲	○	●
Includes requirements on funding of the open data strategy and/or open data initiatives	○	○	○	○	●	■	■	■
Includes requirements to monitor the implementation of open data plans/strategy and/or open data initiatives	■	■	■	●	●	■	■	●
Requires stakeholder engagement to promote the reuse of open government data and/or the creation of an ecosystem of open data users	○	■	○	○	●	▲	■	●

Yes, available in law ●

Yes, available in a decree ■

Yes, available in other instruments (implementation guidelines, recommendations etc.) ▲

Not available ○

Notes. The data presented does not take into consideration Freedom of Information acts.
1. For Argentina, more information is available here: http://servicios.infoleg.gob.ar/infolegInternet/anexos/215000-219999/218131/norma.htm and http://servicios.infoleg.gob.ar/infolegInternet/anexos/255000-259999/257755/norma.htm.
2. For Brazil, more information is available here: http://planalto.gov.br/ccivil_03/_Ato2015-2018/2016/Decreto/D8777.htm.
3. For France, more information is available here: www.legifrance.gouv.fr/affichTexte.do;jsessionid=AE6CD34C644E37D99FD9D1C23BC3F98E.tplgfr38s_2?cidTexte=JORFTEXT000033202746&categorieLien=id and www.legifrance.gouv.fr/affichTexte.do?cidTexte=JORFTEXT000029463482&categorieLien=id and www.legifrance.gouv.fr/affichTexte.do?cidTexte=JORFTEXT000024072788.
4. For Germany, more information is available here: www.gesetze-im-internet.de/egovg/__12a.html.
5. For Korea, more information is available here: http://law.go.kr/engLsSc.do?menuId=0&subMenu=5&query=%EA%B3%B5%EA%B3%B5%EB%8D%B0%EC%9D%B4%ED%84%B0%EC%9D%98%20%EC%A0%9C%EA%B3%B5%20%EB%B0%8F%20%EC%9D%B4%EC%9A%A9%20%ED%99%9C%EC%84%B1%ED%99%94%EC%97%90%20%EA%B4%80%ED%95%9C%20%EB%B2%95%EB%A5%A0#li Bgcolor0.
6. For Mexico, more information is available here: www.dof.gob.mx/nota_detalle.php?codigo=5382838&fecha=20/02/2015 and www.dof.gob.mx/nota_detalle.php?codigo=5397117&fecha=18/06/2015.
7. For Peru, more information is available here: http://138.197.48.84/dkan/img/DS-016-2017-PCM_Datos_Abiertos.pdf and http://138.197.48.84/dkan/img/Guia_RapidaDAG.pdf.
8. For the United States, data refers to the H.R.1770 - OPEN Government Data Act bill. More information available at www.congress.gov/bill/115th-congress/house-bill/1770/text.
Source: OECD (forthcoming), *Open Government Data Report*, OECD Publishing, Paris.

In Korea and the United States, these instruments set mandates to define chief data officers positions across public sector institutions with specific responsibilities in order to encourage institutions towards OGD-driven public value creation. In France, the Digital Law specifically requires that data on gas and energy consumption be provided as open data (National Assembly and the Senate, 2016). Data taxonomies are equally identified in the Executive Decrees on open data published in Argentina and Brazil (OECD, 2017b).

In Germany, the E-gov Law established a central agency with the responsibility of providing advice to public authorities regarding the publication of data as open data. The German law also defined an accountability mechanism for the open data policy, therefore mandating the federal government to report to the Parliament on the progress and publication of OGD by public sector authorities at the federal level.

In light of the above, the Mexican government may consider implementing the following policy recommendation in the long term:

- Strengthen the national legal framework for open government data in the country and consider the development of a specific law on open government data that could be useful to support policy continuity:
    o In light of potential reforms for the institutional governance model for OGD, this instrument could also be used to define the new institutional governance model (see the Recommendation on "Institutional governance", above).
    o It would also contribute to providing further clarity to the relevance of specific elements relevant for the OGD policy in Mexico (including institutional CDOs, policy monitoring and evaluation mechanisms, development of open data strategies by selected line ministries) and in line with priority national interests (e.g. sector-specific data taxonomies, and data governance for public sector productivity).

From policy goals to a structured path: Developing an open data roadmap

The inclusion of open data as one of the key enablers of the 2013-18 National Digital Strategy stresses the connection and contribution of OGD to broader policies and sets the strategy to promote the use of open data for the achievement of key policy goals (e.g. the contribution of OGD to land management improvement, the digital economy and natural disasters' prevention and mitigation are clearly stated as part of the National Digital Strategy). Broader policy objectives are also included in the Open Data Executive Decree (e.g. promotion of economic development, competitiveness, accountability, citizen participation, government efficiency and better public services) and highlighted as action lines of the 2013-18 Programme for a Modern and Closer Government (e.g. in support of sectoral policies such as health) (see "Mexico in the context of the OECD work on open government data", Recommendation 3, above).

The need to deliver results (in conjunction with the institutional and funding model for open data) led the General Direction of Open Data to define a set of actions to generate quick policy wins in line with the aforementioned policy goals. As a result of this process, the Office of the President was able to respond to the challenge of aligning the open data policy with high-priority policy issues in the country.

For instance, initiatives such as Próspera Digital (a public programme for technology-driven social inclusion) capitalised on the opportunities brought by open data and data-driven policy making for the reduction of maternal mortality (see "Mexico in the context of the OECD work on open government data"). The construction of the New International

Airport for Mexico City and the use of the Open Contracting Data Standard to monitor procurement processes are also examples on how OGD increasingly embedded strategic policy priorities, such as social inclusion and anti-corruption outlined in the Modern Government Programme and the National Digital Strategy.

In Mexico, the activities of the Office of the President focused first on organisational learning (e.g. by developing policy tools such as the Implementation Guide and open data standards), institutional capacity building, open data publication through the central open data portal, and then in the delivery of policy results aligned to the national priorities.

All of the above was possible following a test-and-learn approach that ensured the openness of the General Direction of Open Data to continuously learn and scale up impactful open data practices while also identifying and setting up key strategic partnerships with actors at the international level and from the still maturing national open data ecosystem. As a result, OGD was driven by an agile and entrepreneurial model that enabled self-learning, flexibility and experimentation within the Office of the President. This was needed to ground policy goals through the implementation of specific open data initiatives; bring clarity to the course of action to be followed; and increasingly embed the Office of the President's overall vision for open data across the broad public sector (see "Mexico in the context of the OECD work on open government data").

Together, the Office of the President and the Ministry of Public Administration carried out considerable efforts to deliver policy achievements. Nonetheless, there is a need for continuous efforts in the future to keep increasing policy maturity across the public sector. These efforts need to be supported by a policy framework that enables the selection and prioritisation of new initiatives to the stated overarching goals in a more systematic and structured fashion if Mexico wants to secure the long-term sustainability of its open data policy's results.

A more structured and well-defined approach to support sustainable policy implementation will be needed in the mid term. This would contribute to ground the implementation of open data initiatives towards long-term policy implementation. For instance, The 2012 United Kingdom's Open Data White Paper[5] set a clear policy vision and defined the strategy to be followed by the United Kingdom in terms of the instrumentation of the OGD policy. The UK strategy centred on three core areas of work: open data's enhanced access; building trust; and, the smarter use of data across the whole public administration. Each of these core themes included a set of strategic objectives and the rationale of its contribution to the achievement of goals in core areas of work.

The above also requires bottom-up initiatives and actions from different actors of the ecosystem propelling ideas, initiating activities, but also taking up clear responsibilities all along the life of individual initiatives, thus strengthening the networked system of accountability – essential to securing sustainable results. Sharing use cases and good practices beyond those initiatives led by the public sector is crucial to further strengthen the case for OGD and the evidence-informed support to advance the OGD policy in Mexico. One interesting example observed in France around the central open data portal used as a platform for value co-creation and knowledge-sharing platform where all user communities can not only upload data and promote reuse to develop apps or services (OECD, 2015), but foster ecosystem networks having the French government as a provider of such a collaboration space. This approach enables proactiveness from different actors and the building of a stronger open data community whose ideas can be used to inform the OGD policy with a crowdsourcing and collaborative intelligence approach.

In this respect, Mexico could benefit from the implementation of the following policy recommendations in the medium term:

- Sustaining the clear connection between open data, public sector modernisation, the digital agenda, national development and sustainable development goals would be necessary to ensure the relevance of the open data and digital government as an enabler of broader policy goals.
- Capitalise on the experience and knowledge acquired so far in relation to the OGD policy and develop a national open data roadmap framed in line with the overall digital agenda and the National Digital Strategy in the country:
  - o Towards 2019, it will be necessary to define a more specific course of action for the open data policy, and highlight how policy goals will be operationalised, achieved, by whom and who will be involved in the implementation process. Bringing further clarity to the objectives of the open data policy and its operational process (e.g. using open government data as an actionable policy instrument) requires setting clear lines of action – such as the ones included in the Modern Government Programme - identifying allies and champions, and empowering these actors.
  - o The development of the strategy would benefit from an open and inclusive process where stakeholders from the public, private and third sector, the academia and the media can provide inputs and co-design the strategy in collaboration with the chief data officer. This process would also contribute to building further buy-in from these actors and provide legitimacy to the process. The strategy should be perceived as a multi-stakeholder, collaborative and crowdsourcing exercise led by a coalition of actors, including the Mexican government, with a common interest in open data and shared policy goals.
- Further connecting the open data initiatives with other sectoral policies and vice versa, beyond its discernible ties with the National Digital Strategy, would contribute to ensuring the maturity of open government data in Mexico. While the digital agenda would be perceived as the main policy driver of OGD efforts, the inclusion by default of open data as part of other sectoral policies should be further explored. These strategic efforts should serve as an evidence basis to inform the development of the open data strategy in the medium term:
  - o The current efforts on the publication and use of open data for anti-corruption should be sustained across political administrations. Preventing and identifying corruption in the public sector is a priority for the Mexican government. Efforts at the national (e.g. open procurement data) and international level (e.g. the implementation of the Anti-Corruption Open Up Guide of the International Open Data Charter by the Mexican government) should be further advanced.
  - o Scale up the use of open data and digital technologies for natural risk management policies, including prevention, emergency response and reconstruction. The actions taken by the Coordination of National Digital Strategy as part of the emergency response actions after the 7.1 Earthquake that hit Mexico City on 19 September 2017 showed evidence on the potential of OGD in regard to civil protection policies. There is a need to formalise the use of open data and digital technologies as part of emergency response protocols as part of civil protection policies. Further co-ordination with the

Ministry of the Interior and the General Coordination of Civil Protection would be beneficial in this respect.

The role of public sector institutions: Data stewardship

In Mexico, the public sector open data ecosystem is still maturing. Open government data is in the process of being fully understood as a key component of the public sector data value chain - and as such, as a key strategic asset for the public sector – and the result of efficient public sector data governance models rather than being a separate policy. A culture of solving policy problems with data is not yet widespread across the public sector beyond the efforts of the General Directions of Open Data and Innovation. This might be a symptom of the lack of a strategic understanding and approach to OGD across the entire public sector, and a focus on data publication as the overall and final goals instead of an intermediate step.

Evidence from the OECD mission to Mexico indicates that most data administrators and institutional existing profiles do not fulfil the role of institutional chief data officers neither *de jure* nor *de facto*; thus their activities are mainly focused on: 1) deciding what data to open up; and 2) making data publication feasible in line with the requirements set by the Office of the President and other technical guidelines produced by the INEGI (the Mexican National Statistics Office).

Results from the OECD Open Government Data Survey 3.0 suggest that the impact of a chief data officer within the central/federal government is underpinned if such a strategic role is mirrored by the availability of institutional chief data officers in each ministry and/or agency. The availability of institutional chief data officers (iCDOs) reflects data stewardship and improves overall policy performance. The mismatch between a chief data officer within the central/federal government and the lack of data stewardship within public sector institutions undermines the possibility of further scaling up the understanding of open data from mere technical matters or beyond a data publication approach.

In Mexico, the understanding and responsibilities of institutional chief data officers need to be redefined and formalised in order to maximise the public value of open government data and leverage data as a strategic asset. Institutional chief data officers should guide institutions in understanding the strong positive value associated with the publication and reuse of their open data and steer their efforts in this regard. In turn, they should link with their equivalents across the different groups of the ecosystem to increase awareness and interest to promote the strategic use and reuse of open government data in a co-ordinated manner, so as to foster synergies and linkages. This will be essential in the context of Mexico, as results from the survey to institutions indicate that the lack of value proposition and the lack of public interest are the main obstacles institutions face to open up their data.

Countries could benefit by ensuring that the stewardship at the institutional level mirrors the central role in a systemic and integrated fashion. Chief data officers and institutional chief data officers go hand in hand to ensure the strategic implementation of data governance and open data strategies, therefore maximising data availability, data accessibility and data reuse. Mutual co-operation is necessary to ensure co-ordination. As such, the data governance of the data value chain requires a clear, strong and co-ordinated leadership at all levels in order to be effective, efficient and deliver results.

In line with the above, the Mexican government may consider the following policy recommendations:

- In the medium term, follow the trend observed among other OECD countries and work towards the appointment of institutional chief data officers (or positions with this role) across line ministries (e.g. such as stated in the Open Data Law in Korea and the US OPEN Data Bill). The increased availability of iCDOs would contribute to scaling up inter-institutional co-ordination to the strategic level. Institutional chief data officers need to promote the use of data for strategic policy, sectoral and institutional objectives while ensuring strategic data governance models within public sector institutions. The value of open government data must be exploited across institutions, and more broadly across the ecosystem, and iCDOs should stand as the main advocates to that purpose:
    - In the short term, the appointment of iCDOs would benefit from the development of a job profile (e.g. definition of required skills and competencies for this and other roles, i.e. technical positions) as done by Korea and the United Kingdom.[6] This would avoid the capture of such a strategic role by in-house technical-level professionals. The current efforts on developing an open data competency standard in co-operation with CONOCER (see "Towards a data-driven public sector", Recommendation 4, above) should be capitalised on as an opportunity to move beyond the mere definition of highly technical data-related competencies.
- In the medium term, create a collegial body as an institutional mechanism to secure engagement and co-ordination of the iCDOs at the strategic and the technical level (such as the Sub-committee of Open Data of the Ministry of Public Administration, and the Specialised Technical Committee on Open Data of the INEGI). This would sustain co-operation and secure co-ordination across the administration, as well as the engagement of key actors at all times (e.g. policy definition and implementation) for efficient and effective implementation, and the fostering of a sense of ownership and shared accountability

Skills, data and the ecosystem as instruments of policy maturity and sustainability

Hand-holding: Sustaining capacity-building efforts within the public sector

The Open Data Squad is under-staffed; therefore, its capacities to manage the requests for support from public sector institutions and citizens are limited. Furthermore, this creates risks of continuity for their role as intermediaries and managers of the ADELA Platform, which has been pivotal in constantly improving the central open data portal. While the new version of the ADELA Platform will reduce the need for the Squads to participate in the data publication process (e.g. the platform will apply data harvesting functionalities to collect data from public sector institutions in an automated fashion), there is still a need to further build overall capacities and awareness of the relevance of "data as a policy instrument".

The new version of the Open Data Implementation Guide (published on December 2017[7]) focuses on increasing data accessibility and reusability, which requires central guidance on technical matters. Yet, the lack of stewardship inside public sector institutions hinders the capacity to connect open-data-related efforts with the achievement of institutional goals (e.g. improving service delivery and increasing productivity) and of sectoral policy objectives (e.g. transport, health, agriculture).

Experiences from other OECD countries (e.g. Norway, Sweden)[8] with extremely vertical governance models have shown that guidance and support from the centre are needed to orchestrate an effective policy implementation at the agency/public institutions level. The lack of such an approach increases the risk of fragmented, siloed and dispersed efforts by agencies and the subsequent absence of clarity in terms of needed actions.

The Mexican government could consider implementing the following policy recommendations:

- In the short term, prioritise the sustainability of the Open Data Squads to sustain the efforts aiming to build OGD systemic knowledge within the Mexican public sector. This includes securing the adequate availability of human capital and funding to ensure sustainability in the mid and long terms, and avoid the temporary or permanent cessation of the activities of such a key player.
- In the short and medium terms, sustain the efforts and co-operation with key actors such as the Ministries of Education and Finance for capacity-building activities. Open learning online tools and platforms (e.g. massive online open courses [MOOCs] and MexicoX) and collaboration with civil society organisations (CSOs) (e.g. Socialtic's School of Data)[9] should be further capitalised on as instruments to further build public sector intelligence:
  - Further linking these instruments with formal certification and performance evaluation processes (e.g. defined by the Ministries of Public Administration, Finance and Education) would contribute to ensuring the inclusion of the development of open-data-related skills as a mandatory element of specific competencies and performance measurement frameworks.

Data as a strategic asset: From data infrastructure to data as *infrastructure*

Public sector data assets are neither fully catalogued nor used by public sector actors. When existing, efforts are mostly linked to open government data and not to the strategic use of data within the public sector, therefore affecting the development of a data-driven public sector in the long term.

Open government data remains an isolated policy, often disconnected from the overall data value chain and data governance model across the public sector. While on a conceptual basis OGD is connected to Mexico's digital agenda, in practice the policy is separate and still understood as a policy running in parallel to other efforts clearly linked to digital government policies, such as data interoperability.

On the other hand, building a systemic understanding of the relevance of data *as* infrastructure is necessary to increase awareness of the value of open government data as a strategic asset for the public, private and third sector value chains.

When published and reused, OGD becomes a strategic asset of data-driven business models and creates economic, social and good governance benefits. In this context, data publishers and data consumers play a key role in terms of policy sustainability, such as:

1. ensuring the continuous flow of those data becomes a long-term compromise to be assumed by public sector institutions due to the potential negative implications for data-driven business models resulting from restricted and/or irregular OGD publication
2. increasing bottom-up sustained users' demand for OGD becomes a driver of policy sustainability by itself as such a demand exerts pressure on public sector institutions to sustain the publication of open data (see "Contributing to policy

sustainability through an increased data availability, accessibility and reuse", below).

In consideration of the above, the Mexican government could consider the implementation of the following policy recommendations in the mid and long terms:

- Further develop data architecture and data governance models supporting streamlined inter-institutional data-sharing practices in line with the overall digital transformation of the Mexican public sector, and in connection with the open data policy. Examples from OECD countries like Denmark, Norway and Sweden show how, for instance, the development of information and data governance and management models for the public sector - and the development of basic data registers - could serve as a basis for data-driven public value creation:
  - In this respect, it is necessary to keep building the understanding of the role of public sector institutions as data users, hence placing the needed emphasis on inter-institutional public sector data sharing.
- Sustain the efforts aiming to strengthen the value of the IDMX data infrastructure for all actors in the ecosystem and the value of the IDMX for policy sustainability:
  - Two-way consultation processes led by public sector institutions (and not only by the Office of the President) should continuously inform the IDMX in a structured fashion, i.e. the IDMX informing the institutional open data plans and the reverse. This, together with efforts to engage public institutions in the definition of the IDMX infrastructure, would contribute to building institutional ownership of this policy instrument.

Contributing to policy sustainability through an increased data availability, accessibility and reuse

The quality of open government data is often questioned by users in the Mexican OGD ecosystem. While some efforts have been made to improve the functionalities available on the central open data portal (e.g. data visualisations and a developers-specific section), ensuring the discoverability and accessibility of the data available on the portal is indispensable to make these data useful for users.

Evidence collected during the OECD mission interviews to Mexico City in October 2017 underscored the fact that demand for open government data in Mexico is increasing. As a result, ensuring the quality of the data available in the portal should be a priority in order to keep building the relevance of the central portal as a knowledge platform.

In addition, the increasing demand for OGD might be a sign of a maturing open data ecosystem in Mexico. The case of INEGI (the Mexican National Statistics Office) is a clear example of the value of specific datasets for users. Until 2012, the INEGI followed a for-profit funding model; thus, geospatial data was not open, nor made available for free. As a result of moving towards an open data model, downloads of INEGI's maps went from 5 000 per month (2012, fee model) to 20 000 downloads per month by October 2017. The FINTECH bill introduced in October 2017 is also evidence of the growing digital ecosystem in the country and how the government is handling this evolution (see "Open data and the data-driven economy", above).

The increased demand for OGD and the incremental digitisation of the Mexican society and economy provides a stronger business case supporting OGD investments in the public sector.

In line with the above, the Mexican government may wish to consider the implementation of the following policy recommendations:

- In the short term, enhance data availability and accessibility (e.g. through higher discoverability) to increase data demand and reuse. The user-friendliness of the central OGD portal should be further tested and redesigned to ensure its usefulness for all users. Data accessibility, and in particular its discoverability, remain a challenge. The data are often difficult to find and understand. Implementing complementary efforts (e.g. visualisation) to increase the quality of these data is fundamental to increase data accessibility. Metadata should be understood as an instrument to bring further clarity to OGD, not as an additional element adding complexity.

- In the short and medium terms, sustain the efforts to build capacities among external actors such as journalists, civil society organisations and data-driven companies. This should be perceived as a policy priority by the Mexican government and as the result of a sustained collaboration effort with other public sector institutions, drawing upon the success of specific OGD initiatives (e.g. RetoMX).

- In the short and medium terms, aggregate data demand through collective efforts that involve all actors in the data ecosystem. While maintaining existing close ties and collaboration with some key external actors, the Mexican government would benefit from a user mapping exercise to assess the state of the OGD ecosystem and identify new players beyond those already actively engaged:
  - The development of an open and crowdsourced user directory should be considered by the Mexican government in order to enable the ecosystem to inform the open data policy in an actionable and continuous fashion.
  - The role and involvement of major private sector players should be perceived as an opportunity to elevate the business case for open data in Mexico. The sustained and increased collaboration with these actors as data users - alongside their role as service providers – would be beneficial to better understand the use of OGD in the macro sense. Yet, the private sector community, as seen in CSOs, should also acknowledge its own responsibility as for-profit data users and use this negotiation power to contribute to policy sustainability.

- In the medium term, further develop the central OGD portal as a platform for co-creation of OGD and collaboration among different stakeholders, following the practice of other OGD champions across the OECD, such as France. At the moment there is an untapped opportunity to recognise the relevance of the portal as a space to strengthen the sense of community and as a platform for the different actors of the OGD ecosystem to interact and collaborate needs. The portal could become a vehicle and space for more bottom-up initiatives to flourish. This recommendation complements all the previous ones concerning the need to create more capacities, awareness and demand-driven initiatives, thus lightening up the significant commitment of the Office of the President and of the Ministry of Public Administration.

- In the medium term, explore the implementation of government-led seed funding models to invigorate the demand. The current funding model of some business and civic start-ups (receiving funding from well-known organisations) may put at risk the continuity of their work. There is a need to invest and develop business models that require seed funding in the short term, but can self-capitalise in the mid and long terms:

- o The implementation of a diversified funding mechanism would benefit data-driven civic and business innovation. While efforts to use the public sector as a lever of data-driven business models have been tested by the Mexican government (e.g. by providing economic rewards through Retos Públicos, or using funding from the National Institute for Entrepreneurs), seed funding efforts should be further explored and sustained.
- o If implemented, monitoring and evaluation of the benefits generated as a result of these exercises should be enforced during all stages of incubation (from seed funding to post-incubation results and sustainability).

Monitoring actions and delivering results to support policy sustainability

While there is clear evidence of the willingness of the Mexican government to implement monitoring initiatives in relation to open data publication by public sector institutions monitoring, data causality models and clear policy monitoring and evaluation mechanisms need to be established. These are needed not only for consistent monitoring and evaluation but also in relation to results' communication and dissemination.

In line with the above, the Mexican government could consider the implementation of the following policy recommendations in the short term:

- As presented in the 2016 review, data request formats could be used as data collection instruments to monitor user-specific data reuse. The new data request functionality included on the central OGD portal could be improved in this respect by following the examples of other OECD countries like the United Kingdom. As such, this functionality could include additional fields aiming to keep track of who is using the data, for what purpose and the expected benefits of such reuse. This information would be useful to map the ecosystem and monitor success cases of data reuse.
- Sustain an open-by-default approach for the development of ranking and monitoring tools for data publication. Public sector openness leads to public sector accountability by empowering OGD users and citizens to monitor policy developments and spurring peer-to-peer monitoring. The current provision of institutional rankings measuring data publication by public sector institutions should be sustained in order to further develop and/or add new features related to the compliance of national and international commitments, such as the Sustainable Development Goals (SDGs) and in connection with other efforts such as www.agenda2030.mx.
- Communicate and show the results of the OGD policy and initiatives as key to sustaining momentum:
  - o Follow the example of other leading OECD countries like Spain[10] and perform an assessment exercise to identify, map and disseminate successful practices on data reuse contributing to the creation of public value. This would benefit the business case for open data, and expand the mapping of actors and practices at the central and local level.
- In the medium term, the development of the open data roadmap (see "From policy goals to a structured path: Developing an open data roadmap", above) itself should be perceived as a collaborative policy evaluation process to communicate, assess, evaluate and obtain feedback on the results of the OGD policy in the

country so far. This exercise would contribute to prioritising those elements that require utter attention by the Mexican government (e.g. affecting an effective policy implementation), which should be addressed by the open data plan. The participation of the ecosystem in this process would be crucial.

- In the medium term, establish an accountability mechanism to report on the advancements of the open data policy in a regular, open and proactive fashion. Different institutions/public entities involved in the implementation of the open data policy should report on a regular basis (e.g. yearly, bi-annual) on their advancements and achievements to the authority in charge of co-ordinating the OGD policy. This reporting mechanism should be open and ensure accessibility by all actors of the open data ecosystem.

Notes

1. Institutions' responses to OECD (2017a), "Follow-up Survey to the 2016 Open Government Data Review of Mexico", Question 47. ¿Qué acciones se pueden llevar a cabo actualmente para fortalecer y dar continuidad a la Política de Datos Abiertos?

2. For more information see www.modernisation.gouv.fr/documentation/decrets/une-nouvelle-organisation-pour-la-transformation-publique-et-numerique-de-letat-decrets-du-20-novembre-2017.

3. For more information visit www.gov.uk/government/publications/government-transformation-strategy-2017-to-2020/government-transformation-strategy-better-use-of-data.

4. Institutions' responses to OECD (2017a), "Follow-up Survey to the 2016 Open Government Data Review of Mexico", Question 42. Indique el origen de los fondos utilizados para la puesta en marcha de la estrategia de datos abiertos institucional.

5. For more information see the 2012 UK Open Data White Paper available at https://data.gov.uk/sites/default/files/Open_data_White_Paper.pdf.

6. See for instance the description of positions included on the Korea Open Data Law as part of the 2016 OECD *Open Government Data Review of Mexico*, and the description of technical data-related skills developed by the UK government available here: www.gov.uk/government/collections/digital-data-and-technology-job-roles-in-government.

7. For more information, see www.diariooficial.gob.mx/nota_detalle.php?codigo=5507476&fecha=12/12/2017.

8. See, for instance, OECD, 2017c.

9. For more information, see https://es.schoolofdata.org/.

10. For more information, visit www.ontsi.red.es/ontsi/sites/ontsi/files/Casos%20de%20%C3%89xito%20y%20Mejores%20Pr%C3%A1cticas%20en%20la%20reutilizaci%C3%B3n%20de%20informaci%C3%B3n%20p%C3%BAblica%202016.pdf.

References

Government of the Republic of Korea (2016), "Act on the Promotion of the Provision and Use of Public Data", English version provided to the OECD by the Korean government.

HM Treasury and The Rt Hon George Osborne (2015), "Spending Review and Autumn Statement 2015", London, www.gov.uk/government/publications/spending-review-and-autumn-statement-2015-documents.

National Assembly and the Senate (2016), "Loi n° 2016-1321 du 7 octobre 2016 pour une République numérique", www.legifrance.gouv.fr/affichTexte.do;jsessionid=47281A01B2C38AA0CF434A EA987A516F.tplgfr36s_1?cidTexte=JORFTEXT000033202746&categorieLien=id.

OECD (forthcoming), *Open Government Data Report*, OECD Publishing, Paris.

OECD (2017a), "Follow-up Survey to the 2016 Open Government Data Review of Mexico", OECD, unpublished survey.

OECD (2017b), *Compendium on the Use of Open Data for Anti-corruption: Towards Data-driven Public Sector Integrity and Civic Auditing*, OECD, Paris, www.oecd.org/gov/digital-government/g20-oecd-compendium-open-data-anticorruption.htm.

OECD (2017c), *Digital Government Review of Norway: Boosting the Digital Transformation of the Public Sector*, OECD Publishing, Paris, http://dx.doi.org/10.1787/9789264279742-en.

OECD (2016a), "OECD Open Government Data Survey 3.0", OECD, www.oecd.org/gov/2016-OECD-Survey-on-Open-Government-Data-3.0.pdf.

OECD (2016b), *Open Government Data Review of Mexico: Data Reuse for Public Sector Impact and Innovation*, OECD Publishing, Paris, http://dx.doi.org/10.1787/9789264259270-en.

OECD (2015), *Open Government Data Review of Poland: Unlocking the Value of Government Data*, OECD Publishing, Paris, http://dx.doi.org/10.1787/9789264241787-en.

Office of the Prime Minister (2015), "Extrait du Bleu Budgétaire de la mission : Direction de l'action du gouvernement", www.performance-publique.budget.gouv.fr/sites/performance_publique/files/farandole/ressources/2015/pap/pdf/DBGPGMPGM129.pdf.

Ubaldi, B. (2013), "Open Government Data: Towards Empirical Analysis of Open Government Data Initiatives", *OECD Working Papers on Public Governance*, No. 22, OECD Publishing, Paris, http://dx.doi.org/10.1787/5k46bj4f03s7-en.

US Congress (2017), "OPEN Government Data Act", www.congress.gov/bill/115th-congress/house-bill/1770/text.

Further reading

Mexican government (2015), "Informe de Actividades del 15 de Julio al 27 de Octubre de 2015: Implementación de la Política de Datos Abiertos, Escuadrones de Datos Abiertos".

Mexican government (2015), "Infraestructura Estratégica de Datos Abiertos".

Mexican government (2014), "Acuerdo por el que se aprueba la norma técnica para el acceso y publicación de datos abiertos de la información estadística y geográfica de interés nacional" [Open Data Technical Norm for National Interest Information, Open Data Technical Norm for National Interest Information, National Institute of Geography and Statistics, *Diario Oficial de la Federación*, 4 December, www.dof.gob.mx/nota_detalle.php?codigo=5374183&fecha=04/12/2014.

Mexican government (2013), "Programa para un gobierno cercano y moderno 2013-2018" [Close and Modern Government Program], *Diario Oficial de la Federación*, 30 August, www.dof.gob.mx/nota_detalle.php?codigo=5312420&fecha=30/08/2013.

Mexican government (2013), "Plan Nacional de Desarrollo 2013-2018" [National Development Plan 2012-2018], http://pnd.gob.mx.

OECD (2016), *Digital Government in Chile: Strengthening the Institutional and Governance Framework*, OECD Publishing, Paris, http://dx.doi.org/10.1787/9789264258013-en.

OECD (2014), "Recommendation of the Council on Digital Government Strategies", adopted by the OECD Council on 15 July 2014, OECD Public Governance and Territorial Development Directorate, www.oecd.org/gov/digital-government/Recommendation-digital-government-strategies.pdf.

Annex A. Summary of recommendations by timeframe for implementation

	Short term (<1 year)	Medium term (1-2 years)	Long term (>2 years)
Governance			
Institutional governance		Institutionalise and formalise the positions of a chief data officer and chief digital transformation officer within the Office of the President	
		Consider the creation of a digitalisation agency in charge of co-ordinating the digital agenda in the country, including digital government, open data and public sector innovation policies	
		In line with other OECD countries, consider the creation of a dedicated fund on open data for the entity/authority/function in charge of defining the open data policy and co-ordinate its implementation	
Policy funding		Increase the involvement of the Ministry of Finance (MoF) in terms of policy implementation	
		Create/envisage a specific budget line in the institutional budget dedicated to the overall digitalisation of the public sector, including the sustainability of the open data policy	
Legal framework			Strengthen the national legal framework for open government data in the country and consider the development of a specific law on open government data that could be useful to support policy continuity
Structured policy implementation		Sustain the clear connection between open data, public sector modernisation, the digital agenda, national development and the Sustainable Development Goals	
		Capitalise on the experience and knowledge acquired so far in relation to the OGD policy and develop a national open data roadmap framed in line with the overall digital agenda and the National Digital Strategy	
		Further connect the open data initiatives with other	

	Short term (<1 year)	Medium term (1-2 years)	Long term (>2 years)
The role of public sector institutions: Data stewardship	The appointment of iCDOs would benefit from the development of a job profile	sectoral policies and vice versa, beyond its discernible ties with the National Digital Strategy, in order to contribute to ensuring the maturity of open government data in Mexico The current efforts on the publication and use of open data for anti-corruption should be sustained across political administrations Scale up the use of open data and digital technologies for natural risk management policies, including prevention, emergency response and reconstruction Follow the trend observed among other OECD countries and work towards the appointment of institutional chief data officers (or positions with this role) across line ministries Create a collegial body as an institutional mechanism to secure engagement and co-ordination of the iCDOs at the strategic and the technical level	
Skills, data and the ecosystem as instruments of policy maturity and sustainability			
Hand-holding: Sustaining capacity-building efforts within the public sector	Prioritise the sustainability of the Open Data Squads to sustain the efforts aiming to build OGD systemic knowledge within the Mexican public sector Sustain the efforts and co-operation with key actors such as the Ministries of Education and Finance for capacity-building activities		
Data as a strategic asset: From data infrastructure to data as infrastructure		Further develop a data architecture and data governance models supporting streamlined inter-institutional data-sharing practices in line with the overall digital transformation of the Mexican public sector, and in connection with the open data policy Sustain the efforts aiming to strengthen the value of the IDMX data infrastructure for all actors in the ecosystem and the value of the IDMX for policy sustainability	
Contributing to policy sustainability through an increased data availability, accessibility and reuse	Enhance data availability and accessibility (e.g. through higher discoverability) to increase data demand and reuse Sustain the efforts to build capacities among external actors such as journalists, civil society		

Short term (<1 year)	Medium term (1-2 years)	Long term (>2 years)
organisations and data-driven companies		
Aggregate data demand through collective efforts that involve all actors in the data ecosystem		
	Further develop the central OGD portal as a platform for co-creation of OGD and collaboration among different stakeholders, following the practice of other OGD champions across the OECD	
	Explore the implementation of government-led seed funding models to invigorate the demand.	
Monitoring actions and delivering results to support policy sustainability		
As presented in the 2016 review, data request formats could be used as data collection instruments to monitor user-specific data reuse		
Follow an open-by-default approach for the development of ranking and monitoring tools for data publication		
Communicate and show the results of the OGD policy and initiatives as key to sustaining momentum.		
	The development of the open data roadmap itself should be perceived as a collaborative policy evaluation process to communicate, assess, evaluate and obtain feedback on the results of the OGD policy in the country so far	
	Establish an accountability mechanism to report on the advancements of the open data policy in a regular, open and proactive fashion	

ORGANISATION FOR ECONOMIC CO-OPERATION AND DEVELOPMENT

The OECD is a unique forum where governments work together to address the economic, social and environmental challenges of globalisation. The OECD is also at the forefront of efforts to understand and to help governments respond to new developments and concerns, such as corporate governance, the information economy and the challenges of an ageing population. The Organisation provides a setting where governments can compare policy experiences, seek answers to common problems, identify good practice and work to co-ordinate domestic and international policies.

The OECD member countries are: Australia, Austria, Belgium, Canada, Chile, the Czech Republic, Denmark, Estonia, Finland, France, Germany, Greece, Hungary, Iceland, Ireland, Israel, Italy, Japan, Korea, Latvia, Luxembourg, Mexico, the Netherlands, New Zealand, Norway, Poland, Portugal, the Slovak Republic, Slovenia, Spain, Sweden, Switzerland, Turkey, the United Kingdom and the United States. The European Union takes part in the work of the OECD.

OECD Publishing disseminates widely the results of the Organisation's statistics gathering and research on economic, social and environmental issues, as well as the conventions, guidelines and standards agreed by its members.

OECD PUBLISHING, 2, rue André-Pascal, 75775 PARIS CEDEX 16
(42 2018 25 1 P) ISBN 978-92-64-29793-7 – 2018